The
Bitchy
Waiter

The *Bitchy Waiter*

Tales, Tips & Trials from
a Life in Food Service

DARRON CARDOSA

STERLING
New York

STERLING
New York

An Imprint of Sterling Publishing
1166 Avenue of the Americas
New York, NY 10036

STERLING and the distinctive Sterling logo are registered trademarks
of Sterling Publishing Co., Inc.

ISBN 978-1-4549-1724-3

Distributed in Canada by Sterling Publishing Co., Inc.
c/o Canadian Manda Group, 664 Annette Street
Toronto, Ontario, Canada M6S 2C8
Distributed in the United Kingdom by GMC Distribution Services
Castle Place, 166 High Street, Lewes, East Sussex, England BN7 1XU
Distributed in Australia by Capricorn Link (Australia) Pty. Ltd.
P.O. Box 704, Windsor, NSW 2756, Australia

For information about custom editions, special sales, and premium and
corporate purchases, please contact Sterling Special Sales at 800-805-5489
or specialsales@sterlingpublishing.com.

Manufactured in Canada

2 4 6 8 10 9 7 5 3

www.sterlingpublishing.com

Contents

When I say "my pleasure," you should
know that the "I hate you" is silent.

appetizer

noun. • A small dish of food or a drink taken before a meal or the main course of a meal to stimulate one's appetite; something to begin with.

GREAT MAN ONCE SAID, "IF EVERYONE COULD just wait tables for six months of his life, the world would be a better place." I am almost certain those words came from the mouth of Plato in 325 BCE, but it may have been my friend Jane, who said it in 1994 when we waited tables together in Times Square. Regardless, I do believe that if more people put on an apron and did their time as a server, the world would be a more patient and understanding place. I am a waiter and have been one for over twenty years. Contrary to what people often think, it is my "real job." It is a job that takes skill, flexibility, a keen mind, and an incredible amount of patience.

As "eating out" has become one of America's favorite pastimes, you would think that more people would have respect for those of us who take their order, bring their food, and make sure their dining experience is a good one. Sadly, that is not the case. Many customers look at their server as someone who is beneath them. How else would you explain the customer who snaps his fingers to get my attention and then ignores me to answer his cell phone when I get to the table? Or the parents who ask me to turn off the television over the bar that is showing the big game because they don't allow their kids to watch TV while they eat? Or when I tell people that the restaurant only carries Pepsi® and then they ask me if I can run to the deli to get them a Coca-Cola®? These people clearly have never worn an apron and carried a tray for tips. If they had, they would know how to treat their servers.

Many people think the job is easy and only for those who have no education, skills, or ambition. They are wrong. Many of us have degrees. From real colleges. I have even worked with people who have graduate degrees but chose to wait tables because the money can be good and maybe that MFA in Shakespearean acting didn't open up jobs the way they expected it to. Contrary to popular belief, waiting tables can be a very stressful job. If you don't believe me, you can ask a former coworker of mine named Rhonda who once disappeared from her station. She was eventually found curled up in the fetal position and crying under the pay phone near the restrooms. The stress of having a full section of people all screaming that they needed their chicken fingers right away proved to be too much for poor, poor Rhonda. Of course the customers had a point. After all, they had tickets to "Teletubbies Live" at Radio City Music Hall, and with the show starting in thirty minutes, Rhonda's sanity was simply not a priority for them. We servers wiped away her tears and finished her shift for her because we were all in that hot mess together.

Do I expect a federal mandate to be issued requiring everyone to wait tables for six months just so they can see what it's like on the other side of the menu? No, but I do wish that more customers could take a moment and put themselves in my shoes—my horribly ugly, slip-resistant shoes, which I am required to wear, but which my employer won't pay for. Waiting tables is a profession that deserves more respect than it gets, but I guess it's hard to earn respect when you smell like a fajita skillet and there is honey mustard in your hair.

On occasion, I look at myself and question where I gained my stellar attitude toward my service job. How did I imbibe such a healthy outlook for working in a restaurant? I flash back to the mid-1980s. Madonna is on the radio, Cabbage Patch dolls are all the rage, and a girl at school wears a pair of red jelly shoes every day. I am sixteen years old, and I've just gotten my first job ever. For $3.35 an hour, I work as a dishwasher at one of the premier dining establishments in all the land, the finest place to enjoy a high-quality steak that was cooked to perfection and served to you with a smile. Okay, not really. It is a family-style buffet steakhouse in Victoria, Texas. You knew it was fancy because it had a salad bar with three different dressings.

I took the job because two of my best friends worked there as waitresses. They made all the money, while I toiled in the back, emptying grease traps, taking out garbage, and mopping bathrooms. But I was in the food and beverage industry, and knew I had found my home. I did not deal with customers very often, except when someone spilled something and I had to go out into the dining room to clean it up. Within my first week, I knew that the job was a piece of crap, but the money! Fifteen hours a week at $3.35 an hour was bringing me about 35 bucks a week after taxes. I was rich! Rich, I tell you!

One night, someone wanted chicken fried steak without gravy. The person must have either been from someplace other than Texas or *non compos mentis* because everyone knows that in Texas, chicken fried steak is eaten with gravy on it. That's just how it's done. It went out to the table with gravy, and the customer gave it back to the waitress, who gave it back to the kitchen staff, who then gave it to me, the dishwasher.

"Wash that gravy off that meat," my manager told me. "They don't want it."

I thought they were playing a joke on the new kid. I laughed nervously, not sure what to do.

"Uh, what? Wash the meat?" I asked.

"Wash that gravy off that meat. Never mind, I'll do it myself."

My manager sighed with dissatisfaction and took the spray nozzle from my hands. He held the chicken fried steak with his other hand and sprayed the gravy off it, then threw the soaking-wet piece of meat back onto the plate. I stared at him in disbelief as he tossed the meat into the fryer for a few minutes and then pulled it out, put it on a fresh plate, and handed it back to the waitress, who took it back to the table and served it just as the customer wanted it: chicken fried steak with no gravy.

I learned that night that we in the food service industry have a responsibility to make our customers happy. Whether it is giving them a warm smile, making sure they have the perfect ambience, or even something as simple as washing the gravy off their meat, we are there to please. I thank you, steakhouse manager, for teaching me how important it is to make sure the customer is always happy.

I quit three weeks later because according to my diary, the job was "interfering with my social life." Several years later, when I was a busboy at a Mexican restaurant in Denver, my diary spelled out my future: "September 30, 1989. Worked tonight and made $31. Cool, eh? People tell me I'm a great busser. I want to be a great waiter. I really do."

Be careful what you wish for . . .

TODAY YOUR ENTRÉE COMES WITH A SIDE OF MY BITTER TEARS.

entrée

noun. • The main course.

CHAPTER ONE

THE CUSTOMER IS *NOT* ALWAYS RIGHT

THERE IS AN OLD SAYING THAT "THE CUSTOMER IS always right." I beg to differ. There are times that customers are completely wrong and have no idea what they are talking about, but after years of hearing that they are always right, it has filled them with the delusion that people in the service industry can't possibly know what they are doing. I think that the service industry has done itself a disservice by continuing to let customers manipulate employees. Believe it or not, customers, sometimes your waiter is right.

Death by Cabernet

I thought I poisoned someone at work. For a brief second it seemed as if I was going to have to use my years of watching *St. Elsewhere, Grey's Anatomy*, and *General Hospital* to cobble together some type of medical rescue. A woman at Table 15 practically went into anaphylactic shock when she tasted a bottle of wine she ordered and found it to be "horrific." What a fucking drama queen.

She wants to order a bottle of red wine for her table of four but she has a friend at the table who doesn't like red wine, so it is a bit of a challenge. The lady informs me that she is a wine representative, so apparently she knows everything there is to know about the fermented grape. She is intent on discovering a bottle of red that her friend can tolerate. Personally, I think they should order one bottle of red for the three of them, and the one person who wants white wine can just order it by the glass. But, no, she decides on an organic California Cabernet, and she asks if her friend can taste it first to make sure she likes it. Fine. Her friend tastes it and says it is good, but what the hell does she know? It's been established that she does not like red wine. When I show up to the table with the bottle, I uncork it and pour a bit for Miss Wine Rep of America. She swirls it around in her glass and then smells it about a 150 times and finally lets it flow over her very sophisticated palate. After she swallows, she makes a face as if I have accidentally served her the bottle of gasoline that we keep right next to the bottles of Cabernet. She shakes her head back and forth as if she is having a seizure, her hair whipping about and her lips puckering all the while.

"Wow! Wow! Wow! Whew . . . uh, okay. Well . . . that is a really strong alcohol content. It's like the wine just slapped me in the face."

God, how I envied that wine.

"I assume that means you don't like it?" I query.

"No. It's okay. I think the bottle just needs to air out a bit. It's fine, it's fine." Judging by her reaction, it isn't anywhere close to fine. But she says it's fine, which is fine with me.

"Are you sure?"

Saying you're allergic to something and being allergic to something are two different things.

She swallows hard and says, "It's not you. It's the bottle."

Bitch, I know it's not me. Did you see my ass stomping grapes in California in 2009? I ain't got shit to do with this bottle of wine. All I did was carry it from the bar to your table and then open it.

She insists she will drink it, but after five minutes, she calls me over and tells me that it is impossible to drink because it is "so horrific." She offers me a sip to confirm how *repellant* it is, but I tell her, "I'm good. I like vodka." She sends the bottle back and orders a bottle of what they had already been drinking at the bar as they waited for their table. Good idea, lady.

The rest of the bottle that is so awful goes back to the bar, where our manager tastes it and deems it perfectly fine. It is then sold by the glass to another table, which also seems to think it is more than adequate. The chef and the manager both agree that this is the wine rep's attempt to convince us that our wine selection is poor and that *she* is the one who can fix the problem—if only we would buy from one of her labels. Fat chance, wine rep. You have pissed off the manager with your theatrics, and he has vowed to me that he will never consider sampling your wares. You lost that game, honey. However you did win something:

And the award for best overreaction to a taste of wine goes to . . . Miss Wine Rep of America at Table 15! Congratulations! You can take this bottle of 2009 Cabernet and shove it up your Pinot Noir.

Bloody Mary Whine Bag

It's been a while since I have had a real bitch in my station, one so bad I needed to vomit out my feelings about her, but tonight at the club, she slides into Booth 1 to hear the performer of the night. I only have one nerve when I get to work, and this bitch has to get all up on it. She is wearing a lot of makeup, like Tammy Faye (may she rest in peace) levels of makeup. And she is wearing a black top that has sequins on it. It may have had some feathers around the collar, too. I'm pretty sure it did, but I have already tried to erase her image from my memory, and parts of the night are gone forever. The loss of memory may or may not have something to do with the alcohol I consumed after work.

"How's the Bloody Mary?" she wonders, when I ask what cocktail she would like.

I act as if I have tasted one before and say that it is delicious. They get ordered all the time and no one ever returns them, at least. People really think that I have tasted every cocktail on the menu? Do my customers think that I sit around at work and drink every night? Okay, maybe they *do* know me, but I have never tasted a Bloody Mary because that would involve a vegetable serving, and I try to avoid those at all costs. I bring her a Bloody Mary, and, later on, when it is time for the second required drink, she whispers to me that the Bloody Mary was awful and she will have a Cabernet instead.

After the show, she calls me over to again let me know that the Bloody Mary was horrible.

"Oh, I'm sorry," I say. And I am sorry she didn't like her drink because I know it is expensive. "Another lady tonight had two, and she really enjoyed them."

"Well, it was horrible," she says with disgust in her eyes.

"I guess it's a subjective opinion then. I'm so sorry."

End of story . . . so I think.

"No, I'm a bartender and I know. There was no vodka in it. It was just tomato juice and horseradish."

She is wrong, of course. I know for a fact that it had vodka in it. I watched it being made and we simply don't leave liquor out of drinks. I give her the check, and she looks at the $45.73 total and gasps. "Is the tip included?"

"No, ma'am."

She shoots me a look that says, "Are you freakin' kidding me?" She gives me a $20 bill and a credit card and tells me to put the twenty to the check and the balance on the card. I take her credit card receipt back to her with a total of $25.73 on it and she looks at it and snorts with dissatisfaction.

"No, I want to put twenty in cash and then the balance on the card!"

"I did that, ma'am. Twenty dollars cash plus $25.73 totals $45.73. I believe that is the total of your check, right?"

She looks at it again and then spits out, "Fine!" like she is doing me a favor. Look lady, I didn't fucking invent math. Do I look like Pythagoras? Pay your bill and let's move on.

On the way out, of course she has to let the bartender know that the Bloody Mary was horrible and that she is a bartender and she knows best and blah, blah, blah . . . I don't get what her deal is. If she didn't like the drink, she should have told me at the beginning. The lady at the next

booth sent her vodka-and-cranberry back so we could add more juice (because we apparently had poured *too much* liquor). I hate when people complain after it's too late to do anything about it, and they won't accept an apology, and they just keep bitching about it.

This lady is a windbag. A big gassy bag of wind that has Bloody Mary and Cabernet breath and is rocking a black sweatsuit-looking ensemble with sequins and fucking feathers. 'Nuff said.

A Pocketful of Peppermills

A restaurant I once worked in made the mistake of offering comment cards to every table. The problem with comment cards is that people are much more likely to fill one out when there is something to complain about, rather than taking the time to offer a compliment. At the end of the night, it is always fun to see what wonderful suggestions people came up with to make our business run more smoothly. One of the ideas really stuck in my craw—and I need to discuss it further because, quite frankly, my craw is tired of having things stuck in it. The suggestion comes from Ellen who farted out this thought when she was sticking a Q-tip® too far into her ear canal:

Why is it that a peppermill must be brought and administered?
For a few hundred bucks, why can't a restaurant just set one out at each table?

Does she think that peppermills grow on trees? Does she have any idea how expensive that would be? She honestly thinks that a few hundred bucks will cover the cost of supplying every table with its own private peppermill? Customers have notoriously sticky fingers—and I'm not just talking about what they got on their hands from the sugar caddy that I never wiped clean from Sunday brunch when that baby covered it in syrup and played with it. Women like Ellen would be stuffing those peppermills into their purses, bags, and any other orifice just so they could get home with a fancy new, complimentary peppermill. I can see it now. Every morning when it is time to reset the tables, half the peppermills would be missing. It's hard enough to maintain creamers in a restaurant without them disappearing, so I can only imagine that peppermills would fly outta the place like hotcakes.

At my restaurant, we have four peppermills. I never suggest freshly ground pepper because I feel that the way the food comes from the kitchen is the way the chef intends it to be, and it does not need any other seasoning. Additionally, I'm too lazy to go get the peppermill and walk all the way back to the table. If customers want fresh pepper, they have to specifically ask me for it. One of our peppermills is about two feet high. I assume it's that big so that women like Ellen can't discreetly drop it into her shopping bag and go home with it. It's gigantic. As I am administering pepper onto a plate of tilapia for a customer, I let my mind wander and imagine ever so gently clubbing him over the head with it. It's seriously big enough to do some damage to a skull. All of a sudden I

Asks for extra bread and then puts it in her purse.

am playing my own game of Clue®, but instead of Colonel Mustard in the library with the candlestick, it is Darron the Bitchy Waiter at Table 7 with the peppermill.

So, no, Ellen. Restaurants are not going to start giving every table their own personal peppermill just because you think it is a good idea. Thanks for your suggestion, though. If you see Ellen anywhere, make sure you tell her that her idea is stupid. How will you know it's Ellen? You can't miss her. She'll be the one who asks for extra bread only to put it into her purse. She will be the one who never leaves a sugar caddy without first pilfering every packet of sweetener. She's the one who eats three-fourths of her burger and then tells you it is overcooked and she wants it taken off her bill. She's the one who asks for the early-bird special, even though you don't have an early-bird special at your restaurant. She's the one who asks for a new bottle of ketchup that hasn't been opened yet. She's the one who asks for an extra miniature bottle of maple syrup, even though she hasn't finished her first one. She's the one who will try to stuff a peppermill in her girdle if it means that she can sneak it out of the restaurant without having to pay for it. You know the type? If you see her, you might consider clubbing her over the head with a pepper grinder.

Hold Your Horses, Horse Face

At the club, the show I am working is pretty much sold out, so we are crazy busy. I have a five-top of older women who all seem pleasant enough, with the exception of one lady who must not have been laid since the repeal of Prohibition. Her face is all scrunched up in a permanent scowl, with lips pursed and brow furrowed. At the end of the night, they give me three credit cards and want $62 put on one of them and the balance divided among the other two. No problem. I take the cards to the computer and divide up the check but, in my haste, I make a division error that puts unequal amounts on the two cards. Not realizing my mistake, I return the credit cards to the table and tell them I will be right back to pick them up. Moments later, I see them waving at me frantically, as if their very lives depend on my prompt assistance. I rush to the table, and they explain that their checks are all wrong, so I begin to scrutinize the receipts and figure out my mistake. The woman who appears to be the most tense is getting all bent out of shape, and steam starts to shoot out of her ears.

"I'm sorry, I'm sorry," I say. "I figured it out. I just put in the wrong total and it's totally my fault. The credit receipts have not been finalized so just tear them up. I will void them from the computer, and if you give me your cards again, I will run them correctly."

I am completely honest about it being my fuckup and offer to fix it right away, but ol' tightly wound-up Bitch Face is like, "What? Now, I have to give you my card again? Why, why, why? I already gave it to you!" One of her friends tries to calm her down by telling her to chill out. I think she should try rubbing her nose like they do to a horse when it gets spooked. She has the face of a horse, doesn't she?

I get back to their table a whole two minutes later, but Horse Face acts like I have traveled through three different time zones. As soon as I get there, she whinnies at me that she needs to leave. It must be time for her feeding, and there is a pile of hay somewhere with her name on it.

"Okay," I respond. "I just need you to sign the slip."

She shakes her tail to swat at a fly that isn't really there and says, "I need to go right now."

A friend of hers explains that I need her to sign again before she gallops off, but she protests, "Why, why, why?"

I have had it. I go right up to her long face and say, "Did I ruin your night? Did I just ruin your night? Did you just sit through an hour and a half show with an amazing performer, have a wonderful time with your friends, and then I made a simple error on your credit card, which I fixed, and now you're going to let that ruin your whole evening? Please. Don't let this ruin your night. Just sign the receipt and everything will be fine."

Her four friends back me up.

"Yeah, it's okay, Seabiscuit."

"Relax, Black Beauty."

"What's the big deal, Secretariat?"

"Take a chill pill, you horse-faced bitch of a whore. I hate going out with you. You're such a pain in my neck. Tell your jockey to ride your ass home and feed you a carrot and a sugar cube and shut the hell up." (I may have paraphrased a bit . . .)

Horse Face ekes out a half smile because I have made her realize how petty she is being, and if she continues to act like she has a riding crop up her ass, then she will look like an even bigger horsey bitch.

She smiles, and says, "No, you didn't ruin my night."

I smile back and tell her that I am glad that her night isn't ruined. I jab the spur of my cowboy boot into her side, and she shakes her head and trots off toward the exit. As her friends follow behind her, they each give me a look of apology with a glint of gratitude for putting up with their friend, Flicka.

Cucumber, the Other White Meat

There is a new trend sweeping the country that is going to affect servers everywhere, and it is truly horrible. In a never-ending attempt to stay cool, hip, forward, and chic, restaurants have started to do something that will make people feel like they are eating at some fancy-ass restaurant or spa instead of their local chain eatery. We servers have all dealt with the beer limes and the soda lemons, and now it seems it is becoming increasingly popular to put cucumbers into glasses of water. Dear Lord in Margaritaville and all things holy, please say this isn't happening.

I have had cucumber water, and you know what it tastes like? Fucking cucumber water. It was given to me once when I went to get a massage. You know the routine. The spa attendant hands you your robe along with some paper flip-flops, and says, "Would you like anything to drink, sir (or ma'am)?" I answered water, and the next thing I knew there was a big glass of chilled water in my hand with a goddamn fucking cucumber slice floating in it.

Why don't I want this disturbing trend to continue? Allow me to explain: Servers already have enough to do before the restaurant opens, and I do not want "slicing cucumbers" to be one more thing on the ever-growing list of opening sidework. Isn't it enough that people want lemon in their water and cherries in their sodas and olives in their martinis? Let's leave the cucumber out of it. Besides, I cannot for the life of me understand why anyone would want to put one in their H_2O. It was probably some snooty bitch who first tried it.

> **LADY:** Excuse me, waiter, but do you have any cucumber sandwiches? I missed my afternoon teatime and I am simply dying for one.
>
> **WAITER:** No, ma'am. We don't have any cucumber sandwiches.
>
> **LADY:** And please cut off the crusts first. I cannot stand crusts on my cucumber sandwiches.

WAITER: *Yeah, we don't have any cucumber sandwiches.*

LADY: *And serve it on a lace doily, please. Don't you agree that everything simply tastes better when it is served on a lace doily?*

WAITER: *Um, yeah. I'd put your cucumber sandwich on a doily if we had cucumber sandwiches or Doilies, but we don't. Would you like to try our Buffalo Wing Quesadilla Pizza Potato Pie instead?*

LADY: *Just the cucumber sandwich on the doily, thanks.*

The waiter heads to the kitchen and is all, "This crazy bitch thinks I'm gonna make her a fucking cucumber sandwich. Hey, Salad Guy, hand me a cucumber slice, will ya? I'll show her what I think about her fucking cucumber sandwich."

He takes it to the bar and pours a glass of water and then drops the cucumber into it. He goes to the snooty lady, puts on his biggest shit-eating grin, and places the glass onto the table.

WAITER: *My most sincere apologies, but at this time our chef is unable to prepare your cucumber sandwich, and I just used my last doily when I served an English tea biscuit to the Queen of England sitting at Booth 4. However, I took the liberty of placing a fresh slice of cucumber into a glass of our finest purified water. I hope you enjoy it.*

LADY: [takes a sip] *Why, this is delicious! This is my new favorite beverage of all time; it's so light and refreshing! I'm going to have this from now on at every restaurant I ever eat in, and I am also going to encourage every lady I know to do the same thing. Thank you, waiter. Will you please get cucumber slices for everyone else in my party right away?*

How to piss off your waitress:

I KNOW IT'S NOT ON THE MENU, BUT...

The waiter mentally stabs himself in his heart because he knows he has just created a cucumber monster who will spread this ridiculous notion across the country.

Dear Bitchy,

I need your advice. I work at a bar and grill, and for whatever reason people constantly ignore the HUGE Please Wait to Be Seated sign and mosey on in and seat themselves. I have tried very hard to be nice when this happens, but it has become a daily occurrence and I just can't take it anymore! What would you do?

> Signed,
> Alicia

Dear Alicia,

Oh, this problem again . . . with these buckets of Thousand Island® dressing that we call customers. No matter how HUGE the sign is, they will not read it. They will ignore it the same way they ignore menus, their children, and my crushed dreams. I once worked a restaurant with a patio with a HUGE sign that said, Please See the Hostess If You Would Like to Sit Outside. People constantly sat directly under the sign, paying no mind to it. Even if the sign had been lit up with neon and sparklers and had photos of naked men and women on it, they would ignore it. It's their way.

What can we do? Here is what I suggest: When someone sits down at a table without being seated there by a hostess, ignore the fuck out of them just like they ignored the fuck out of your sign. I have done this many times, and it's very rewarding. When I see someone sit down without the proper protocol, I walk past them continuously until they practically have to pull their arm out of its socket to wave hard enough to get my attention. They will usually say something all bucket-of-Thousand-Island-dressing-ish like, "Uh, excuse me, but we don't have menus." My reply is then, "Oh, that's odd. I don't know why the hostess didn't give you one when she seated you. I apologize for her behavior; she does this all the time. It may be time to mention it to the manager, so they can get someone in here who knows how to do her job. Thank you for bringing it to my attention. I hope her résumé is updated, because it looks like tonight may be her last night." And then Thousand Island family is all, "Oh, well, we seated ourselves . . . We don't want her to get fired . . . Uh, we're sorry." Then they feel stupid, and it makes me feel better.

Or maybe after sitting there for three minutes, they'll say to me, "Uh, is someone going to take our order?" And then I might reply, "I thought this was so-and-so's table. Have you been waiting long?" And then they will say, "Uh, yeah, for like thirty minutes." And then I say, "He must not realize you are here. Did a hostess seat you or did you seat yourself, because that would make all the difference in the world." And then they mumble, "Oh, well, we sat ourselves here . . ." And then I say, "Aha! Now we know why no one came to take your order. It's because you seated yourselves. You should always wait to be seated by the hostess, so these things don't happen."

Basically, there is no way around people ignoring signs and seating themselves, so all we can do is try to embarrass them enough so that the next time they will wait to be seated. It is highly unlikely that embarrassing them will teach them anything at all, but from our point of view, it is immensely satisfying. Try it. You'll love it.

Mustard and mayo,

The Bitchy Waiter

Separate Checks, Please

I am not perfect. Usually, I am calm under pressure. Challenges roll off my back like water off a duck. People don't get my goat because my goat is chill. I am cool as a cucumber. Enter Table 28, which has gotten all under my skin and on my last nerve. Seriously, I had one nerve when I got to work today, and this group of people has found it—and they are riding it like a pony.

If someone makes a reservation for ten people and they all show up together as a group, I am going to assume that they all know each other. Consequently, I am going to put them all on one check. If they expect otherwise, it is their responsibility to make sure I know. I approach my ten-top to get drink orders, and when I get to the last lady, she asks for a separate check, which is fine because I'd rather know sooner than later, when ten people are throwing money at me and telling me they just want to pay for their two Bloody Marys. When she asks for the separate check, I stop and wonder if all the other folks would want their own checks as well.

"Would it be easier if everyone has a separate check?" I ask the table, which ignores me. I ask again. One man answers on behalf of the table.

"We're all friends. We can settle it ourselves. One check is fine."

Famous last words.

At the end of the night, when I place the bill at Table 28, the lady who has her own check hands me cash and says, "Thank you. Keep the change."

Another lady flashes a $20 bill at me and asks, "How much is mine?"

And so it begins.

"Ma'am, you are included on the bill with your friends."

Suddenly everyone is paying attention to me for the first time all night.

"What? We're all on one bill? Oh my God! That's not good. Oh my God! The sky is falling, the sky is falling!"

Everyone suddenly wants separate checks. I glare at the man who assured me one check was fine. At this point, I have twelve other tables to deal with because the show is over and the whole club is paying their checks at once—and now they want me to split a nine-top?

Deep breaths, calming thoughts.

I explain to them that I will do it, but I will have to deal with my other tables first, since this is going to take some time. They are not having it at all. They get pissed off and have mini-conniptions. Brows are furrowed. Veins are throbbing. Friendships are falling apart before my very eyes. I pick up the check and begin the ordeal of splitting it nine ways, trying to remember what each of them had for their two-drink minimum. They are all in a hurry, of course, and the next thing I know, several of them are surrounding me at the computer and throwing credit cards and money at me.

I give a newly separated check to the hostess, so she can run it out to one woman who is especially irritated. All of a sudden Especially Irritated Woman is standing right next to me.

"I need my check right now, or I'm just going to leave," she yells at me.

"Oh, I just had the hostess take it to your table, ma'am."

"Well, I'm *here* now. Go get it," she says.

"It's at your table, and I am trying to divide up these other checks."

"Well, you'd better go get it because I'm leaving."

Resisting the urge to strangle her, I say, "Okay, let me stop what I am doing so I can go get your check, which is at *your* table, where I told you I would bring it to you."

I go to get her goddamn fucking check and come back and place it at the counter beside her.

"Here you are. I will be *right* back."

I go downstairs and sit down for exactly five minutes with my head in my hands. I need to collect myself. If I don't do it, I am going to say something I will regret, and then she will go home and write a horrible review about me and get my ass fired. When I come back upstairs, I see she has left a pile of cash, meaning she did not need change, which is what six out of the ten people did as well. They could have all done that without me separating the check.

The man who assured me one check was fine meekly approaches me at the bar to pay for his check. "I'm *really* sorry for all my friends. I've never seen them act that way. I'm so embarrassed."

Sometimes the only thing that gets me through my shift is the shift drink I will have when it's over.

"Well, I don't like getting yelled at by people when I didn't do anything wrong. I asked if separate checks were better and you specifically told me that one check was fine. This was *not* my fault."

"I'm really sorry. Here, just take this. Take all of it."

He presses $40 into my hand and sheepishly walks out of the club. I look down at the two wrinkled $20 bills and then look at his receipt, which is for $40.29. Not only did he stiff me, but he also shorted me twenty-nine fucking cents.

Hello, My Name Is . . . Why Bother

Some restaurants require the old "Hello, my name is Ashley and I will be your server tonight" routine. I have worked in those places, and I hated it, because announcing my name was always way more trouble than it was worth.

"Hello, my name is Darron and I'll be your server tonight."

"Oh, hello, Darrell."

"No, Darron."

"Oh, Derek? Like Derek Jeter??"

"No, Darron, like the guy on *Bewitched* who was married to Samantha, but I spell it with an O."

"Oh, Darron with an O! That's interesting. Were your parents hippies?"

"Never mind. Hello, my name is *John* and I will be your server tonight."

I have never been a big fan of having to give out my name to customers because I have also found that when I tell customers what my name is, many of them get too comfortable using it and start asking for too much. Thankfully, I never worked at one of those places that has butcher paper on the tables with crayons for the children. Some of the servers write their names on it as they introduce themselves. Once I went to a place where the waitress wrote her name in cursive upside down so that it was facing me. It was very well done and quite remarkable, but don't ask me to spell out my name in cursive, much less upside down. I don't give out my name unless asked.

Since I work at a very small neighborhood restaurant, three blocks from my home, several of my customers *do* know my name. I suppose I don't mind it too much, since I bump into them at the grocery store and I'd rather they say hello to me by name than say, "Hello, Asshole." When people ask for my name, they always follow it up with their names, which I promptly delete from my memory bank. If I remember the names of all my customers, how will I ever remember that episode #109 of *The Facts of Life*, where Jo began her own pizza-making company, aired on October 3, 1984, and was called "Slices of Life"? The memory cells I have left are quite valuable to me, and I must be selective as to what they are used for.

One regular who comes in always thinks my name is Eugene. My name is nowhere close to Eugene. I once played a Eugene in a high school play about Halloween, but that is where my connection with the name ends. I have told her my actual name many times, and she always tells me that I look just like Gene Wilder. The next time she comes in she has forgotten my name and calls me Gene instead, so I correct her. I see her once outside a bar in our neighborhood, and she yells out across the street, "Hello, Gene." I correct her once more. I see her yet again at another bar, and this time she calls me Eugene. I imagine that her train of thought went something like this: "Oh, what is his name again? I know I know it. He looks like Gene Wilder but I know his name isn't Gene. Is it Willy Wonka? No, that's not right. Maybe it's Dr. Frankenstein . . . Gosh, I dunno. I got it!"

"Hello, Eugene!"

I correct her one more time.

She comes into the restaurant a few weeks later and greets us all. She doesn't say my name, and I am happy that at least she isn't calling me Eugene. When she leaves (after three glasses of wine), she gives me a hug and kiss and slurs out, "Wonderful to see you again, Eugene." I am done correcting her. I don't care. I don't know her name, even though she has told it to me often. The difference is that I don't just make up shit when I see her: "How have you been, Phylicia Rashad? Well, listen, Ms. Bassett, the next time you come in, you make sure to sit in my station, okay, Whoopi?"

I agree with most people who say that customers don't care about the names of their servers, and, since servers don't want to give out their names anyway, can we make a pact that we will no longer do it? Let's be done with it. Let's accept our restaurant situation for what it is: a business transaction between two strangers that will last for about forty-five

I WILL DO PRETTY MUCH ANYTHING FOR A 20% TIP.

minutes or so. It should be just like a prostitute and her john: no names, no pleasantries, and no emotions. We give each other what we want and move on. As long as I give good service and get a 20 percent tip (and not crabs), I'm good.

"Hello, my name is none of your fucking business, and I will be your server tonight."

Yeah, We're Out of That

Coke® is the real thing, right? People love their Coca-Cola, but every restaurant has to make a choice whether to serve Coke products or Pepsi products. Most people prefer one over the other but will settle for either, or I will decide for them and tell them we have whatever it is they happen to want. It's not the end of the world when someone wants a Pepsi and all I can offer is a Coke, is it? I didn't tell them a comet is heading toward our planet and we will all be gone in thirty-six hours. Nor did I serve the last known hamburger in the Western world, and anyone who craves one will have to travel to Asia to get one. I did not just walk by their table to crop-dust and let out a silent but deadly fart as a secret retaliation tactic.

Well, okay, I did do that.

A lady calls me over to her table to give me some dreadful news. "Excuse me, but I ordered a Coke, and this is Pepsi. Can I *please* get the Coke that I ordered?" She says "please" as if I am an imbecile and she has to make it *exceedingly* clear that even though she is being a bitch, she is also being polite.

"Ma'am," I say (I always like to say "ma'am" to rude women who are clearly younger than I am). "We only have Coca-Cola products here, so I can assure you that you are, in fact, drinking a Coke." She inhales deeply and slowly in that way that sounds like a sigh and rolls her eyes at me. "I can tell the difference between Coke and Pepsi. If this is a Pepsi, I would rather you just be honest with me than tell me it's a Coke when I know it's not."

"It's Coke."

She shrugs her shoulders and turns to her friend to give her a look that says something like "This poor dumb waiter thinks he can fool me." I pick up the glass of Coke and leave.

As it happens, our soda gun is not working, so all of our sodas are being poured out of cans that we have stacked behind the bar. I go to the bar, fill a new glass with ice, grab an unopened can of Coke, and head back to the table ready to make her eat her words, eat some crow, and then take a whiff of the second fart I will be leaving for her.

After setting the glass down in front of her. I pull the can of Coke from my apron, tap the top of it five times, pop it open, and pour it into her glass.

"It's. Coke." I stand there with my arms crossed, waiting for the apology that I know will never come, and she mumbles something. This time, I inhale, but in that way that makes it sound like I am sighing.

"I'm sorry, what?"

She responds with, "Oh. It's in a can. That's why it tastes different."

crop-dusting: When a server intentionally passes gas at a particularly annoying table.

I fart a third time and leave her alone with her precious Coca-Cola.

She really irked me, but I feel victorious because she never says anything else to me for the rest of her meal. I love it when I can prove without a doubt that the customer is not always right, but I return to her table to fart a fourth time for good measure.

It is very troublesome when customers get so bent out of shape because a restaurant doesn't have something they think we should have. Even worse is when we run out of something that is normally on the menu. We don't like it and we don't do it on purpose, but sometimes it happens. One time a man orders a Cobb salad for lunch moments after avocado has been scrawled onto the 86 board, alerting us that we are out of it. I have to let him know that if the lack of avocado is going to ruin the whole aesthetic of his salad, then maybe he should order something else. Well, the lack of avocado is not okay with him.

"You're *out* of avocado? How can you be *out* of *avocado*? Aren't you a *restaurant*? I don't understand how someone could let that happen."

What I don't understand is how not getting avocado in a salad is anything other than "no big deal." Had I told him we had run out of oxygen and we are on our last breaths, sure. Or maybe if we were out of water, that would be weird. But avocado? Move on, Avocado Asshole. I patiently wait for him to let me know if he wants the salad sans avocado or if he will order something else until I realize that his "How could this happen?" question is actual and not rhetorical. He is staring at me, waiting for a response.

"Uh, you know how sometimes at home you run out of milk, even though you didn't mean to? Like, maybe you ate more cereal than usual and then you baked a cake, which took a lot of milk, and before you knew it, you were out of milk? That happens in restaurants, too. I guess more people ordered guacamole than usual, so we ran out of avocados. *That's* how someone let it happen."

He groans with dissatisfaction and then mentions that there is grocery store nearby, like I am going to hop, skip, and jump over there to get him a freakin' avocado. No, sir. If you are so familiar with the location of the grocery store, then maybe *you* should go there, buy the avocado along with everything else that you want in your goddamn salad, and then go home and make it your fucking self. We're out of avocados, so fucking deal with it.

Another time a lady orders a Chinese chicken salad that had been taken off the menu two months earlier. She gasps when I tell her.

"Oh. My. God. I *loved* that salad. How *horrible* is that?"

She looks like she is going to cry. This is a few weeks after 9/11, so I pause and say, "You know, in the scope of world events recently, I would say it's not horrible at all. Would you like something else?"

She shuts up and orders a Cobb salad with avocado and a Coke, both of which we have that day.

Crazy Mashed Potato Lady

Maybe there was a full moon, or maybe the neighborhood insane asylum left the back door open tonight because we had a crazy lady come into the restaurant. As soon as she appeared at the front door, I took out the little notebook that I keep in my apron and started jotting down details because I knew what I would be writing about next.

She is a regular who hangs out at the bar next door and pops over to the restaurant when she wants to chew on something other than ice and cigarette butts. I've never gone inside the bar and, judging from the clientele and the way it looks through the window, I never will. It's one of those places where people drink hard liquor and smoke cigars with one foot outside the door and the other foot inside, so they can drink and smoke at the same time. I imagine if I went in and ordered a Queen's Park Swizzle, I would promptly be asked to leave, much in the same manner that George Bailey and Clarence are escorted out of Nick's Bar in *It's a Wonderful Life*. This woman has come into the restaurant after knocking back a few because she needs something to soak up the liquor in her stomach. She also needs some conditioner and a moisturizer, because the only thing I know of that is drier than her hair and skin is my tongue, but my shift drink is still hours away. She tells us she likes our mashed potatoes, so she wants a side of them. She points to one of the to-go boxes that are sitting behind the bar and slurs out, "I want that size, but fill it all the way to the top."

Now this is a box that ordinarily holds much more than one side dish. It usually houses a side of fries that take up a lot more space than a couple of dollops of mashed potatoes. The owner/chef is near the bar and confirms that she wants the box filled up.

"Yeah, fill it up," she says. Her breath is liable to get a small child drunk if the poor thing were to inhale deeply within a close radius of her.

The owner informs her that in order to "fill it up," it would probably be a total of four orders, but Drunky McDrunk Drunk confirms that she loves our mashed potatoes and she wants them. After the kitchen puts the potatoes in the to-go box, she pays for them and stumbles back to the bar next door to eat the potatoes and pour more cheap beer into her drinking hole. Forty-five minutes later, she calls us, very upset, and I happen to be the one who answers the phone.

"Did I just now pay $17 for mashed fucking potatoes?" she wants to know.

Actually, she paid $17 for mashed potatoes almost an hour ago, but it seems to have taken her this long to process that she handed a $20 bill to the bartender, and he only gave her $3 back.

"Well, you paid for four sides of mashed potatoes to fill the to-go box. Since each side order is $4 plus tax, yes, you did pay $17 for mashed potatoes. But it was forty-eight minutes ago, not just now," I say as I look at the stabbed check to see when exactly she placed the order.

"Who the fuck pays $17 for mashed potatoes?" she yells.

"People who love our mashed potatoes and then order four sides of them, I guess."

"I wanna talk to the owner!"

The owner gets on the phone and reminds her that she specifically asked us to fill the to-go box to the top. He also reminds her that he told her it would be four separate side orders. She is not satisfied and says she is coming back over.

Two minutes later, the Drunken Beauty with a hankering for mashed potatoes appears at the door. She is holding the to-go box and a plastic fork, gripping them with rage. Most of the potatoes are gone with some of them on her shirt and some of them in her teeth.

"I never woulda ordered these if I knew it was gonna be $17," she whines. "Why are they so damn expensive??"

The owner explains to her the simple concept of multiplication and how four times four is sixteen. He also tells her that these are real potatoes, with real butter and real cream, and that they are not cheap to make. She is upset and threatens to tell everyone at the bar next door that we sell $17 mashed potatoes, as if anyone there will remember anything she burps out of her mouth. The owner reaches into the cash register and gives her a $5 bill, apologizing for the miscommunication. The woman looks at the bill and all she sees is another pint of beer. Instantly satisfied with the outcome, she triumphantly turns around to go back to the bar, cradling next to her chest what's left of the potatoes.

"And I'm taking these with me!" she says.

"Have a wonderful night!" I happily chirp. "Enjoy those mashed potatoes and come back real soon!" The sarcasm goes through her as quickly as the beer probably does.

The owner shrugs his shoulders and tells the bartender that the drawer will be $5 short tonight. What will also be short tonight is Crazy Mashed Potato Lady's memory of her mashed potato fiasco, because I'm sure that by the end of the night, the only evidence of it will be a curiously clean to-go container and the aftertaste of beer and spuds.

I Served a Total Has-Been

News flash! I suppose being a "has been" is better than being a "never was," but whatever you are, there is never a reason to be a total bitch to your server. This rant is for that "famous" lady who sat in my station and thought she was still a "somebody":

Look, you had quite the career (key word: *had*). Yes, I knew who you were when you sat down, but I know stupid shit like that. Hell, I know all the names of the actors from every '80s sitcom, and I also know their full character names. I'm a freak like that. Most people have never heard of you.

I'm sorry you didn't like the table we gave you, and it was real cute how you pulled the "Don't you know who I am?" stunt with the host. He did know who you are—sorry, were. And the table he gave you was good enough for Liza Minnelli when she came in, so it should be good enough for your D-List ass. Why so rude?

Maybe it's because you long for the days when you were doing tours of national productions of Broadway shows. Maybe you miss being a guest on *The Ed Sullivan Show*. That must have been very exciting, but let's not forget that it happened fifty fucking years ago, and you are no longer all that and a bag of Funyuns®. Maybe you were in a bad mood because your residual check for your guest-starring role on *The Love Boat* hadn't come in yet. I remember you on that episode. It was 1982 and I thought you were so funny. Your range, versatility, and comic timing were astounding. I am sad that I missed your appearances on *Fantasy Island*. Again, how amazingly versatile you are—or *were*, I mean.

So, you thought you would just go find yourself another table, did ya? Well, we were sold out—oversold, actually—so you can't just plop you F-List ass down at any old table and then make your husband (your fourth, I believe!) carry the drinks over to it. You had a reservation for four people but you sat down at a two-top. Where did you think your two companions would be sitting—in your G-List lap? I must say that I quite enjoyed watching you both slink back to your original table when the host told you to scoot your H-List asses outta there. You seemed irritated when I asked you what you wanted for your second drink, but I was just doing my job. There was no need to snarl your thin upper lip at me and shoo me away as you flipped your hair out of your eyes. Your hair, by the way, looks nothing at all like it does in your headshot, which gives the illusion of hair that is rich and full-bodied and lovely, while in real life it looks limp and lifeless and stringy.

You barked at me to bring the check for you and your husband.

"There are four of you. Is this two separate checks?" I asked.

"Yes! Just bring the check for the two of us. Separate. Checks," you spat out.

"Well, when you make a reservation for four people and you all order together and sit together, I am going to assume it's one check. Give me a minute to split it, and I will be right back."

Golly, you seemed angry that you were going to have to wait while I did that. Were you in a hurry to get somewhere? Did you need to rush home to check your answering service or your beeper to see if your agent called you to be on a reboot of *Lifestyles of the Rich and Famous*? If it came

back and featured you, they should change the name of the show to *Life-styles of Bitches Who Used to Have Careers But Now Nobody Knows Who the Fuck They Are Anyway So They Mistreat Servers to Make Themselves Feel Better about Where They Are in Life*. I would totally watch that show.

Thank you for coming into the club, lady. It's always nice to serve someone I grew up watching on TV. Did you burst my bubble? Not so much. The truth is, I never really thought about what you would be like in person, but now—unfortunately—I know.

Famous Person Dines and Dashes

Recently, I had a walkout. For those of you not in the restaurant business, first off, let me congratulate you on that, but secondly, let me explain what a "walkout" is. It's when someone simply leaves the restaurant without paying the check, knowingly or unknowingly. Depending on the restaurant, it can really hurt the server because very often the cost of that check comes out of the server's apron. It's probably illegal to do that, but it happens all the time, and it's happened to me.

The audience tonight at the club is full of very wealthy people who have come out to support their equally wealthy friend, who fancies herself a singer. I use the term *singer* lightly. Very, very lightly. (If the term were any lighter, it would float away like a balloon filled with helium.) The room is jammed with people who come from money, and they are all entitled, elitist pricks who want what they want, and they want it now. The problem is they don't know how to ask for anything; they only know how to demand.

"Give me a vodka martini," barks out the Lady with Dyed Black Hair.

"Yes, ma'am. Is there any particular vodka you'd like?"

"What? I dunno." She looks around for a friend, a butler, or a maid to make the decision for her. Clearly, someone else usually makes this call. "Just bring me a martini," she spits out.

"Very good. One Belvedere® martini, coming right up," I say, choosing the most expensive vodka on the menu.

Five minutes later, I am sliding past a table while holding a tray of nine beverages. It's crowded and dark, and the tray is wobbling very precariously. Just as I reach my table, I feel someone tapping me on my back. I turn my head to see what kind of medical emergency must be happening that would prompt someone to divert my attention at that precise moment, and a woman tells me, "Vodka tonic." Yeah, these are the people I am dealing with.

At Booth 3, I am waiting on a very famous gossip columnist. She's crotchety and obviously does not really want to be at the show. Seated with her, but on her own check, is the widow of a well-known actor. She's pretty and relatively friendly, especially compared to the royal pains in the asses filling the rest of my section.

"I'll have a margarita, frozen," says the widow with frozen features.

"I'm sorry," I reply. "We can't do frozen drinks because the blender makes too much noise during the show. Is on the rocks all right?"

"Too much noise? Oh." She laughs a bit as if she doesn't quite understand why a blender crushing ice during a musical performance would be any problem at all. "Okay, I guess that's fine."

TOUCHING YOUR SERVER IS A GOOD WAY TO NEVER GET ANOTHER REFILL.

I return with her cocktail. As soon as the show is over, Gossip and Widow get up to make their way out of the room. The gossipmonger's check has already been taken care of, but the widow's has not.

"Ma'am, I have your check. Do you want it now or would you like me to leave it on the table?"

"Just leave it on the table," she tells me.

She never reappears. I go to the hostess, Liz, and ask if she saw them leave. "Yes, they both left. I told them that there was an encore, but the really old one said she didn't care."

"So the blonde lady left, too?" I ask.

"Yeah, why?"

"She didn't pay her check. It was for $45. I just fucking told her I had it, and she told me to leave it on her table."

"Yeah, she's gone."

And now I reach the moral dilemma. Luckily for me, I work in a place where the managers know that these things happen on occasion, and the money does not come out of my pocket. But she should know that what she did wasn't right. Maybe it was an accident and, if that's the case, then she would want to know, right? And if it wasn't an accident, then I should tell the world, so that if other servers see this woman in their section they'll know to acquire a credit card as soon as she puts her *entitled* butt in the seat. What I should do is send this item anonymously to Page Six of the *New York Post* and let the paper publish it, so I can wash my hands of the whole thing. But then again, I like dirty hands . . .

The Softer Side of Bitch

WHAT DO YOU WANT TO BE WHEN YOU GROW UP?

I once heard someone talking about how few people there are who remember what they wanted to be when they grew up. I have always wanted to be the same thing, so it's an easy question for me, but for a lot of people, it's surprisingly difficult to answer. Maybe you wanted to be a fireman or an astronaut or a teacher, and maybe some of you lucky people got to grow up and be just that, as if there were really an astronaut reading this book. But a lot of us are either still striving to fulfill our childhood dreams or we simply don't recall what they were. I asked my mom what she had wanted to be when she grew up, and she had no idea.

"Oh, I don't remember. Maybe a secretary or something."

How could she not know what it was she wanted to grow up to be? I have wanted to be an actor or a writer my whole life and have never stopped wanting it. Over the years, I've gotten lazier about making it happen, but I never stopped knowing that is what I want to be. I briefly flirted with some other career aspirations, including commercial artist, sign maker, and teacher, but for the most part a career in the creative arts was always the one that I clung to. One career I never dreamed about having was waiter, but look what the fuck has happened. Or maybe I *did* want to be one, somewhere deep in my subconscious.

When I was about thirteen years old, my parents felt I was mature enough to stay at home for a few hours at a time and babysit my two younger brothers, Chad and Coby. It was a big deal. One summer, the three of us are all at home and I am responsible for making lunch. I spend the whole morning creating a menu, so we can play "restaurant" at lunchtime. I pull out my calligraphy set and some fancy paper and craft two menus for my brothers. What kind of kid was I that I had a fucking calligraphy set and fancy paper? The same kid who would leave a chocolate on the pillow and place a guest book in my bedroom anytime my grandma would visit and sleep in my room—that's who.

When it is time for lunch, I call my brothers into the kitchen and ask them to sit at the bar. They are presented with menus and get to choose what they want for lunch. The menu consists of macaroni and cheese, peanut butter and jelly sandwiches, or Steak-umms®. For beverages, their options are water, milk, or Kool-Aid®, and, for dessert, I offer cookies or ice pops. This was some fine dining shit. With my mom's apron wrapped around my waist, I try to take their orders. They are having none of it.

"This is stupid. What are you doing?"

"We're playing restaurant, and I'm your waiter. What can I get for you?"

"Whatever. This is dumb," says Chad, who never has any problem telling me that something I am doing is a stupid waste of time or as dumb as fuck. He is ten years old, but he can cut me to the quick like nobody's business. Of course they don't want to let me take their order and then have to sit there and "play restaurant" while I make their Steak-umms and Kool-Aid. They just tell me what they want and get up to go play, knowing full well that I will call them when lunch is ready.

"But, wait. You're supposed to sit and let me *serve* you," I cry out as they run off to play video games or with their Matchbox® cars. "I made *calligraphy menus*," I scream, putting the final nail in the coffin of my restaurant game.

Chad laughs at me, and then Coby laughs, too, because he does whatever Chad does. I am alone in the kitchen. The menus are left on the bar, and I feel stupid for even spending time making them in the first place. They go into the trash can and I take off the apron. I am just the older brother again, making lunch for two unappreciative brats who made fun of me. Lunch is made, they eat it, and I clean it all up. It is the first time I ever serve food to someone who is mean to me and does not leave a tip, but God knows it wasn't the last time.

Did I ever say, "I want to be a waiter when I grow up"? No, I definitely did not, but it happened anyway. Sometimes we end up being something even though we never planned on it. Did the lady at the DMV plan on that job when she was ten years old? Doubtful. Did the postman check that box on career day? Probably not. Did I go to school to be a waiter? Nope. But here I am, a waiter who is writing a book. Sometimes life sends you down a path, and even though there are detours along the way, if we are lucky, we end up exactly where we wanted to be in the first place.

CHAPTER TWO

RESTAURANT 101

MY YEARS IN THE RESTAURANT INDUSTRY HAVE taught me many things—mostly about how to be a better customer when I am dining out. Sometimes, people need to walk in the shoes of others before they can understand what kind of situations others deal with. Since I would never expect anyone to buy a pair of shoes solely for the purpose of learning what it's like to be a waiter, please allow me to share my wisdom with you. If you follow these suggestions, servers will be much less inclined to dislike you, and you may even find yourself getting a free dessert because of your behavior. At the very least, you can be sure that your server won't go home and write a story about you.

LESSON #1: *Use the menu.*

You know what's really annoying about customers? (I mean, other than the fact that they are there in the first place. It would be so much simpler if they cooked at home and just mailed my tips to me.) I hate when people ask for something that is not on the menu. The menu has one purpose and one purpose only: It tells you what the options are in that particular restaurant. If it's not on the menu, it means you can't have it. Plain and simple.

A couple comes in on a busy night. He has a big ol' head and stubby little arms, not unlike Mr. Potato Head. I greet them at the door and inform them that we only have one table left, which is on the patio.

He tells me, "Oh, well, it's just the two of us. We only need one table."

I laugh, thinking he is making a joke, but I see in his face that he is dead serious. (Mr. Potato Head, I am just letting you know that the

The menu has one purpose. Use it!

only table I have available is outside and making sure you are okay with that.) They follow me to the table where I hand them menus. You know, menus? Those things that will tell what you can order for dinner? Mr. and Mrs. Potato Head ask for two glasses of champagne. I imagine they are celebrating that they found her missing ear or that Toys "R" Us' is having a sale. When I come back to the table, they are ready to order.

"Do you have potato skins?" the husband asks.

I look around to make sure I am not accidentally working at one of those tacky restaurant franchises. Once I confirm that there are no televisions playing sports and no guests are eating huge plates of nachos, I know that I am still at the same restaurant I had punched into three hours before. Then I look at his menu to make sure I haven't accidentally given him a pub menu by mistake. Nope, he has the correct menu—the same menu that everyone else has, the one that offers appetizers, such as curry mussels and baked goat cheese with mesclun salad.

"No, sir. We don't have potato skins." My eyes resist their urge to shoot a dagger at the man.

"Oh, that's too bad. Can you make them?"

The cooks don't even like when I ask for the French fries to be well done, and he thinks I'm gonna ask them to make potato skins? Sure, sir. Let me just run to the kitchen and grab some potatoes. I will then scrub them, bake them, slice them, hollow them out, grate some cheese, fry some bacon, fill the skins, bake them again, and then add a dollop of sour cream and sprinkle it with scallions. I'll be back in an hour and thirty minutes.

"No, sir. We can't make potato skins."

Maybe there's another appetizer on the menu that you and your spud of a wife would enjoy, and do not ask if we have a fucking onion blossoms. We don't. Nor do we have Buffalo wings, fried mozzarella, spinach artichoke dip, popcorn shrimp, sliders, or quesadillas, so don't ask for those, either. Look at the menu, choose something, order it, and I will bring it.

They settle on mussels with a side of fries. Every time they put a French fry in their mouths, a shiver of horror runs down my spine because it looks like they are eating one of their own.

LESSON #2: *When I say it's hot, it's hot!*

Dear Customer,

When I tell you something is hot, please believe me. Just because you see me holding a hot dish does not mean that your fingers have the same super-human strength to withstand heat as mine do. You see, I hold hot plates all the time, so my fingers have built up a tolerance to this silly thing called fire. Is it sad that I no longer have fingerprints? Sure, but it allows me to carry plates to your table even after they have sat under the heat lamp for twenty minutes and gotten very hot, so it's all worth it. When your food is ready, the cooks puts it "in the window" under this big strong lightbulb that keeps things nice and warm until I finally get around to bringing them to your table. Your plates will sit there and sit there until you ask me, "Is our food ready yet?" When I hear that question, it is my cue to bring your dishes to you because I like food to sit in the kitchen for as long as possible until I know you really want it. Consequently, your plates get really hot. Because I have been doing this since I was a fresh-faced young boy of twenty, my fingers are callused, angry, and rough. They're just like my heart.

When I approach your table with steaming piles of nachos, wings, or calamari and I say, "Be careful the plate is very hot," I mean it. You don't have to reach out and touch it to verify that what I said is true because you will more than likely burn your hand and then throw me an angry look that you will then have to take back because you will realize I just fucking told you the stupid-ass plate was hot, you dumb bag of hair. Please don't be jealous of this amazing talent I have that allows me to hold hot things, because it really is nothing. The cooks in the kitchen can practically reach into a vat of hot oil with their bare hands to pull out French fries. They can stir pots of soup with their elbows. They can light cigarettes just by touching them with the tips of their fingers. They are the true heroes.

In closing, let me say one more time: When I say something is hot, it is hot. Don't touch it. I will laugh at you when you recoil in pain, and I won't

feel bad about it. I will not try to hide my laugh, either. I will say something like, "See, I told you it was hot. What, you didn't believe me? Let me get you some butter to put on that burn; it will make it all better." And then I will laugh again, because putting butter on a burn to make it better is an old wives' tale that will make it burn more. If you are dumb enough to ignore my warning about a hot plate, then maybe you will be dumb enough to smear butter on a burn.

Mustard and mayo,

The Bitchy Waiter

Dear Bitchy,

I'm an eighteen-year-old college student, and I feel horrible. I was out to dinner with some friends, and I had just given the server my credit card to pay for the bill. We didn't split the bill—my friends paid me in cash—and we had been an all-around undemanding table. While we were waiting for my card to come back, though, one of my friends announced some shocking news, and I completely forgot to sign my slip, tip the waiter, or even pick up my card. I realized this later and went back to sign and tip the waiter, but my card had disappeared. I checked my card activity, and the last charge was our meal the night before. I feel horrible. Any ideas on how to make it up to the server?

> Signed,
> Ashamed

Dear Ashamed,

First of all, you must let go of all your feelings of shame. Let me rephrase that: You must let go of your feelings of shame that have anything to do with this particular incident. Save that feeling of shame for other times like when you turn twenty-one, have too much to drink, and throw up in a planter outside of a strip club in Puerto Vallarta (been there), or when you decide to have sex with someone and then two weeks later you have a family of crabs living in your underwear (been there). There are lots of opportunities for shame, my dear, and this ain't one of them. You are but a child of eighteen and still filled with the wonder and hope that so many of us who are older no longer have. Do not let shame and negativity seep into your life, because once shame makes an appearance, it is ever so difficult to push it away. Be not shameful! It sounds to me like you made an honest mistake and then went back to fix it. If you returned the next day and left a tip, your server was satisfied.

As for your missing credit card, there are a couple of possibilities with that. It is feasible that the server was disappointed that there was no tip or signature, and he "accidentally" lost the card in the nearest trash can. It is also possible that it got thrown into the cash register under the drawer (with all of the other credit cards that have been left behind), and they just couldn't find it. My vote is the "accidentally lost in the trash can."

Of course, the one thing I want to know is what shocking news your friend announced. What words are so surprising that it makes someone forget to sign a credit card, stiff a server, and then leave it all behind? I have some ideas about what your friend might have said:

- I'm pregnant, and the father of my baby is that guy I met on Craigslist® who is a Gemini, likes long walks on the beach, and has twenty-seven piercings and a tattoo of Paula Deen on his ass.

- I think our server is the Bitchy Waiter, and he seems nice but a little bit drunk.

- I have a hedgehog in my vagina.

- I think Donald Trump would make an excellent president of the United States.

- My parents told me that I am adopted and my birth mother is Peggy from Mad Men.

- I am going back to school for a degree in hotel and restaurant management.

Any of those announcements would be enough to unsettle you and cause you to forget to sign your credit card slip. If you already tipped the server, there is nothing else to make up. You have done your part. Carry on with your shame-free life and keep on tipping 20 percent.

Mustard and mayo,

The Bitchy Waiter

LESSON #3: *Don't call me a faggot.*

One of the most common questions I am asked is if I have ever spit in anyone's food. The answer is absolutely not. In my twenty-plus years in food service, I swear on a stack of takeout menus that never once have I ever been so upset with a customer that I felt the need to take his food and spit in it. That is unprofessional, immature, unsanitary, and disgusting, and I would never do that to a plate of food. However, one time I did spit into a glass of lemonade. Although I am not proud of this fact, I admit that I stooped to that level. Blame it on youth, blame it on an eagerness for revenge, or blame it on the rain, but it happened.

I am working my regular lunch shift in the early 1990s in Houston, Texas. One of my tables has four burly truck-driving men who no doubt came in to get their daily allowance of fried food and gravy injected into their veins. In those days, men like that intimidated me with their cowboy hats and all that body hair sprouting from every pore. They are not being particularly nice to me, but I could tell they were never particularly nice to anyone else, either. They are "real men" who think that manners don't matter and that the gruffer they are, the manlier they are. One guy keeps sucking down lemonade because he wants to make sure he takes full advantage of the unlimited refills that are available. As I bring another glass to the table, I distinctly hear the word "faggot," followed by deep, guttural manly man laughs. When I put the glass down, they all look at me and abruptly stop laughing. They continue with their non-use of "please" and "thank you," and when it comes time for yet another glass of lemonade, I have had it.

Still fuming about the "faggot" remark, I regress to high school where I heard that aspersion cast at me as a regular occurrence. Some people had nicknames like Skip, Moose, or Boss. Mine was Faggot. Suddenly these four men at Table 14 represent every boy in high school who had ever called me that word. They are the same boys on the school bus who knocked me down and made me cry. They are the same assholes who scrawled my name on the bathroom wall, saying I give good head. They are the same punks who slashed my tires at the homecoming dance. As I fill up a gigantic glass of lemonade, I hock up a loogie from deep within my tortured soul and debate whether or not to follow through on my sudden impulse for reprisal. (Plus, it's harder than you'd think to find a place in a sidestand where one can safely spit into a glass of lemonade without being seen.) But I do it. I let the spit drop into the glass, and then I stir it with the straw and go back to the table.

"Here you are, sir. Is there anything else you need right now?" He grunts. I step away and watch him drink his lemonade.

What is weird is that I don't feel better, I feel stupid and just as disgusting as he is. What has come over me that suddenly I want to make this one man pay for every wrong that has ever come my way? I give them the check, taking one of the lemonades off the bill.

LESSON #4: *Yes, we know you want cold beer, asshole.*

Everyone wants beer to be cold. It's pretty much expected. That's why there are signs in front of bars that say, ICE-COLD BEER! If the signs said, LUKEWARM BEER! or ROOM-TEMPERATURE BEER! nobody will want to go to that bar. That's why it's so irritating when people order a beer from me and then add "a *cold* one." Really, sir? You want a *cold* beer? Thank you for clarifying that, so I didn't bring you the one that just came out of the oven. A man orders a beer and then gives me a very specific instruction. "Can you get it from the back of the refrigerator and make sure it's the coldest one?" Little does he know, every beer in the reach-in has been there since the night before, so they are all the same temperature. What he also doesn't know is that I don't have the time or physical dexterity to get on my knees and reach all the way to the back just to get the "coldest one." My fingers do not have super-sensitive thermostats on them allowing me to determine which bottle is a tenth of a degree colder than another one. The last thing he doesn't know is that I don't fucking care.

His table is pretty close to the bar, so I know he will be watching to see if I really reach all the way to the back or not when retrieving his beer. I squat down and grab the first bottle of beer I touch but make sure to rattle it against other beer bottles so the clinking sound will register with him as me reaching all the way to the back to get that ice-cold beer he wants. I place it on his table. "This one is really cold," I tell him. "My

When you order coffee, you don't have to specify that you want it hot. It's implied.

fingers are freezing!" He takes a sip and gives me the thumbs-up to let me know it has met his expectations. I wonder what he thinks I would have done if he gave me a thumbs-down. Later, I see his bottle is almost empty.

"Sir, would you like another beer?"

"Yes, I would. Can you make sure you get the coldest one for me?"

Really? So he has to reiterate that he wants a *cold* beer? I am so happy he reminded me because I had just put a six-pack of beer into a pot of boiling water, and I might have accidentally given him one of those, had he not refreshed my memory that he wanted *cold* beer. After all, a whole fifteen minutes have passed and I have completely forgotten his special instructions. He tells me again. "Just get the bottle that's all the way in the back, thanks."

Again, I jingle-jangle the bottles as I pull the beer from the front of the reach-in. "Here you are, sir. I think this one is even colder than the first one!" He takes a swig and gives me the customary thumbs-up. I give him the imaginary finger.

Customers, we know you want your beer to be cold. We also know you want your coffee to be hot. There is no need to verify these things because that is how everyone wants them. We are not going to test ten different bottles of beer to see which one we think might be the coldest one. Same thing with the coffee. The only time your coffee will be "extra hot" is when you are particularly annoying and your server feels the need to take your cup of coffee and put it in the microwave for two minutes so it's a big cauldron of scorching java that will hopefully scald your face off when you take a sip. Yes, I have done that. If I had a subzero super-freezer, I would do the same thing with that bottle of beer that you want to be "extra cold." I would love to serve your bottle encased in a block of ice and say, "I wanted to make sure your beer was as cold as possible, so here's an ice pick."

LESSON #5: *If you choose to sit outside, please realize that is where nature lives.*

This is the story of a lady who hates bugs. She does not like bugs in any way and does not like bugs on any day. Not red bugs or bed bugs, black bugs or white bugs, big bugs or small bugs, wig bugs or tall bugs.

"Oh, I just can't stand them," she'd say. "With their creepy little legs and their beady little eyes, laying all their eggs. I hate them worse than flies."

The lady's name is Betty, and all of her friends know how she feels about creepy crawlers. No amount of discussion can convince Betty that bugs have any purpose in life other than to freak her out.

"But what about ladybugs?" they'd say. "They're so cute. Or roly-poly doodle bugs? Surely you don't mind them."

Betty minds every kind of bug.

One day, Betty makes plans to go out to dinner with her best friend, Joan. Well, Betty *thinks* that Joan is her best friend, but in reality Betty gets on Joan's last fucking nerve, and the only reason Joan tolerates Betty is out of a sense of obligation. You see, they were once very close in college, and their mothers are best friends, but over the years their interests have changed. Betty turned into an exasperating fuck of epic proportions. Still, Joan makes time to have dinner with Betty every four or five months.

The two women arrive at the restaurant, which has a quaint little patio in the backyard.

"Oh, let's sit outside," says Betty. "The weather is so nice tonight. Would you like that, Joan? I just can't wait to share every single thing that has happened to me in the last sixteen weeks, three days, twenty-one hours, and fourteen minutes since we last saw each other. Oh, please say you want to sit outside, dear Joan."

"Yeah, that's fine. Two for outside," says Joan to the bitchy-looking waiter who is standing behind the bar.

The waiter puts down his glass of seltzer and leads the two women to a table on the patio. He places two menus on the table and tells them he will be right back to see what they would like to drink. As they sit down, Betty looks at the garden that is blooming all around them and begins to think of all the bugs that might be crawling around on the plants.

"Are you still freaked out by bugs?" asks Joan.

"Well, I'm better than I used to be," Betty fibs. "I just think this table is a little too wobbly. Let's move to that one over there."

Betty picks up the menus just as the waiter is coming back to the patio to take their drink order. Betty waves at him as if he can't see that they have moved five feet from where they were the last time he saw them.

"Yoo-hoo! We're over here now!"

"Yeah, we had to move because Betty doesn't like bugs," smirks Joan.

The waiter takes their drink orders. Betty asks for a water with extra lemon while Joan orders a dirty vodka martini with extra olives.

"Like, porn star dirty," she says. "And hurry."

As Joan opens the menu, Betty looks down at the cement to make sure there are no bugs that are plotting an attack on her legs. She sees nothing but realizes that she is still too close to the plants.

"Joan, dear, would you mind too terribly if we move to that table over there?" she asks.

"Bugs?" asks Joan.

"No, no, no, it's just that the sun is shining in my eyes and I want to be able to give my full attention to you and not have to be thinking about shielding my eyes as I try to tell you about my love life—"

"Fine," groans Joan. "Let's go. You really need to get past this whole 'bugs are scary' thing."

Betty tries to convince her friend that it is just the sun and the wobbly table, but Joan knows it is because Betty thinks a bug might climb up her leg and sneak into her vagina. At this time the waiter reappears with drinks for the two women.

"Yoo-hoo, we're over here now. Yoo-hoo!! The sun was shining in my eyes at that other table. I swear it wasn't because I thought a bug might crawl up my leg or anything like that."

The waiter pays little attention because all he is thinking about is what kind of shift drink he will be having two hours later. He places their drinks before them, telling them he will be right back to take their food order. He notices how Joan practically grabs the martini off the tray as if she needs it more than oxygen. He understands how she feels and makes his way back inside the restaurant.

Two minutes later, he hears a scream from the patio—a bloodcurdling scream that raises the hairs on the back of his neck. Betty comes running into the restaurant, arms flailing about her body.

"Oh my GOD! A bug just crawled up my leg! Your patio is swarming with bugs! What kind of patio has that many bugs?? Oh my god! Why are there so many bugs out there?" she cries.

"Well, it's outside, so it's kinda their home," replies the waiter, who now seems totally bitchy.

This is when Joan comes inside as well, holding an empty martini glass. She hands a $20 bill to the waiter and looks at her friend.

"Listen, Betty: If you don't want to be close to them, don't ask to sit on the fucking patio. Bugs always find the bitches. I'm outta here."

Joan saunters out of the restaurant, leaving Betty the Bug Bitch alone, embarrassed. Betty straightens her hair, adjusts her skirt, clears her throat, and says, "I do not like bugs in any way and do not like bugs on any day. Not red bugs or bed bugs, black bugs or white bugs, big bugs or small bugs, wig bugs or tall bugs." Then she leaves the restaurant.

"Bugs always find the bitches," says the waiter.

5 Obnoxious Things Customers Need to Stop Doing

1. **STOP SAYING, "IT WAS HORRIBLE" AND "I HATED IT."** Yes, we get that you are being ironic by saying you disliked your meal when your plate is licked cleaner than the balls of a horny hound dog, but do you have any idea how many times servers hear that line? Every time you say it, we have to force out a little laugh to make you feel as if you should go on the road with your new stand-up routine, and then, as we clear the plate, we will say our stupid stock answer, which is something like this: "Wow, I don't even have to send that plate to the dishwasher. Ha, ha, ha."

2. **STOP EXPECTING SOMETHING FREE FOR YOUR BIRTHDAY.** Here is a news flash for you: Everyone in the world was born, and everyone has a birthday. Most restaurants don't care. It's no great accomplishment to be birthed, and it does not merit a free round of drinks or a dessert. It's not going to make a difference if your friend pulls me aside and mentions it or if you show me your driver's license. And while we're at it, stop asking servers to sing "Happy Birthday." Feel free to do it yourselves, but there is no reason for the entire restaurant staff to drop what they are doing and screech out a song just so you can feel important or embarrass your friend. If you want to feel important, apply for a gold credit card, and if you want to embarrass your friend, stand up in the restaurant, point to him, and exclaim, "That is the worst fart I have ever smelled." There is no need to get your server involved. Besides, if you ask your server in New York City to sing, there is a

good chance he's a musical theater actor, and his bitterness about singing to a stranger at Table 12 instead of a Broadway audience may take away any joy you were expecting from the song.

3. **STOP MAKING OUT IN RESTAURANTS.** If dinner is your foreplay, that's great, but let's not make it a threesome. Keep me out of it. No server wants to watch a game of tonsil hockey happening in his station. Public displays of affection are one thing, but groping and fondling each other are another. What's even more disturbing to see is two people who are making out *after* they have eaten. The thought of your girlfriend nibbling on all that New York shell steak that was stuck in your teeth is enough to make me want to toss my cookies into your to-go bag. And just so you know, if you sit on the same side of the booth, I can guarantee you that someone is going to make fun of you.

4. **STOP FIGHTING OVER THE CHECK.** Somebody just pay the damn thing. We find it irritating when you come to us in the sidestand and then slide a credit card into our apron while telling us, "Do *not* let anyone else pay." Too late, sir. Somebody at your table already gave me a credit card with the same instructions, so you lose. When we put the check down, we don't want to see two people playing tug-of-war with it. It's awkward for us to hear you each pleading the case of why you should be paying. "No, I'm a guest at his house, and it's the least I can do" does not concern

me. In addition, "I make more money than he does" is just a terrible thing to say. Whichever credit card touches my hand first is the one that will be used. End of story.

5. **STOP WITH THE CELL PHONES.** We know that you want to take a photo of your enchiladas and post them online right away, but is that really necessary? Can't you put your cell phone away for half an hour so that servers can do their jobs without interrupting your phone call to your great aunt Fanny who wants to tell you all about her bunion surgery? Don't give us dirty looks because you are trying to have a private conversation on your phone and I am standing there trying to take your order. Also, when four people leave their cell phones on the table, those phones take up valuable table space that I may need to, I dunno, place your food on. And every time we fill your water glass, there is the chance that a drop of H_2O may fall upon your link to the outside world. And we don't want to take a picture of you, either. Put the phone in your purse, in your bag, or up your ass. Please.

LESSON #6: *If your party is incomplete, sit your ass at the bar and have a drink until everyone gets there.*

We must discuss the seating of incomplete parties. There are two ways to think about it:

- **Any person who has never worked in a restaurant before:**
  I don't see what the big deal is. I mean, it's not like we're not going to order food eventually . . .

- **Any person who has worked in a restaurant before:**
  Kill me now.

I am at work on a Thursday night and the place is slammed. People in Queens have major cabin fever from being cooped up in their apartments during Hurricane Sandy, and since there is very little subway service into Manhattan, they are settling for dinner at their local joint that has spotty service and a stale menu. We have a 100 percent increase in covers over the last two nights. Slammed.

A woman arrives and alerts us that she is waiting for two or three other people who are "on their way." I ask her if she'd like to sit at the bar and wait for the rest of her party to arrive, but she's says, "No, you can go ahead and seat me now."

I can? I can go ahead and seat you now?? Oh, why thank you, ma'am. My evening is complete because I have had the wonderful opportunity to seat you at this moment.

She wants a booth but, seeing they are full, agrees that she will suffer through the horrible situation of sitting at two small tables pushed together. Never mind that there are millions of people in the area with no heat, water, or electricity.

"If a booth opens up, let me know," she says.

Right, sure, uh-huh. I'm just happy she isn't in my section.

When you arrive at a restaurant and you're in a hurry, it's not your server's problem.

She orders a glass of wine from her server and waits, popping up out of her seat every ten seconds to scan the room for a newly vacated booth. She looks like a fucking meerkat in a pink polyester pantsuit.

About ten minutes later, she is still waiting for the rest of her party. Meanwhile, we are on a waiting list because all the tables are full. One of my booths in the back of the restaurant has paid the check, and they are on their way out. Miss Meerkat smells her chance. She leaves her table at the front of the restaurant and hovers around my booth as I wipe it down. She immediately places her cell phone on the table like she is Christopher Columbus claiming a new territory.

"I've been waiting for this booth, so I'm gonna sit here now," she tells me.

She returns to her original table and gathers her coat, menu, and wine, and then heads back to her little piece of heaven known as Booth 16, where she asks me what the specials are. Now, we have to reset the table in the front and transfer her one glass of wine from the server for that table over to me.

Five minutes later, one of her guests arrives and wants to know what the specials are and order a drink. I regurgitate the soup of the day (verbally, not actually, although the soup of the day is white kidney bean with kale, which sounds disgusting). I go get a Pinot Grigio and then try to carry on with the rest of my tables. Five minutes later, another person arrives at the table, who also wants to know the specials and order a drink. I have now spent an inordinate amount of time on one table. Between transferring the check, resetting her first table, making way too many trips for a first round of drinks, and reciting our laundry list of specials, this table has already gotten more attention from me than I give to some of my family members—and I haven't even taken their food order yet.

"One more person might show up, but you can go ahead and take our order now."

I can? I can go ahead and take your order now?? Oh, why thank you, ma'am. My evening is complete because I have had the wonderful opportunity to take your order at this moment.

Two people are ready and the third only thinks he is. "Hmmm, I don't know. You don't have any fish specials?" he asks me.

"No, sir, the only specials I have are the ones I already told you. Three times."

"Well, what fish do you have then?"

I glare at the menu he is holding, which says we have salmon and tilapia. "We have salmon and tilapia."

Meanwhile, I can see that two other tables in my station are waiting to order, and I also see an order of fries in the window that needs to be delivered.

"Salmon and tilapia, huh? Nothing else?"

"No."

"I wish you had swordfish."

"Salmon and tilapia."

"Okay . . . I guess I'll have a cheeseburger then."

I decide that he will be having it medium with cheddar because, quite frankly, they have used up all of my patience.

This is why I dislike seating incomplete parties. It throws off the rotation of the restaurant, and it always puts us behind because we can't consolidate our trips to the table. Seating incomplete parties requires us to make individual trips to that table over and over again instead of getting all the drink orders in one fell swoop. If you have never worked in a restaurant and still can't understand why seating incomplete parties is a bad idea, kindly go to the beginning of this story and reread it out loud.

LESSON #7: *Theatrics will not make your server like you more.*

When I first see the man sitting at Table 12, my mind flashes back to an old ZZ Top music video from the '80s. The man has a long gray beard that hangs to his chest, and his eyes look possessed, like the evil brother of old St. Nick. When I see his wife reading the menu to him, I remember that I have waited on them before and that the man is blind. I take back the part about his eyes looking possessed, but there is no excuse for a beard like that. It looks like pubic hair on steroids. I recall that this couple is difficult and that the last time they were here, the woman sent her burger back for being overcooked, which is pretty normal since the cook seems to think that well done and medium rare are the same thing. I also recall that they are pains in the ass.

"Hello, folks, how are you tonight?" I ask. "Can I get you something to drink yet?"

She orders an old-fashioned and he looks in my general direction. "I will have a gin martini. Very dry. Up."

"Yes, sir," I say, all the while thinking that martinis are always up. "Would you like an olive or a twist?"

"Yes," he says, and he waits for a laugh from me that never comes. "I also want an onion. I like a salad in my martini." Again, he waits for a laugh that just ain't coming.

"All right, one old-fashioned and a gin martini up with a salad, coming right up."

Minutes later, I place the drinks on the table and watch the man stick his finger in the martini glass to gauge how full it is. They have me recite the specials and then do what most people do, which is decide they don't want a special.

As the man licks his gin-soaked fingers, the woman tells me she is ready to order.

"I'm gonna be bad and order a hamburger," she says, as if this is the first time in her life she has ordered something that isn't the epitome of healthiness. Her ass tells a different story, and it's an autobiography about fried food, gravy, and doughnuts. "I want it medium rare. Will they know what that is?"

"And here we go," I think.

"Well, I know that sometimes they have a tendency to overcook burgers, so I will ring it in as rare so we can cook it more if we need to. Would you like cheese on it?"

"What kind of cheese do you have?"

"We have American and cheddar."

"Oh, I didn't know you differentiated between the two here."

To me, that sounded rude. Am I crazy or did that sound rude?

"Cheddar." Her ass quivers with excitement about the additional calories. "And it comes with fries, right?" Now her ass yelps with anticipation.

ZZ Top informs me he will have the same thing but would like bacon on his.

The woman interjects. "Really? You want bacon on it? It was *hardly* bacon last time."

Now, I *know* she's being rude, so I question her.

"Hardly bacon? What do you mean? Was there not enough of it? Or you didn't like the taste of it?"

"Oh, never mind," she says into her old-fashioned.

I ring in their order, making sure to ask for *rare* burgers, and about thirteen minutes later, their food is ready. I take the burgers and fries to them, and the woman immediately takes a bite of it and discovers it is too well done.

I'LL HAVE THE BACON, DOUBLE CHEESEBURGER, BUT I NEED IT VEGETARIAN AND GLUTEN- AND DAIRY-FREE.

"No. They did it again. This is *not* medium rare." She thrusts the burger toward me so I can get an eagle's eye view of the burger that definitely looks more on the medium side.

I am not pleased. I ordered it rare, and here it is way too done, and now I have to deal with this angry and difficult customer. I agree with her that it is not medium rare and offer to have the kitchen make it again.

"No, I'll eat it, but look at it!" She again shows me the burger. "You look disgusted by it. You must not eat meat. Is that why you have that look of disgust on your face?" she asks me.

I lie and tell her that I very rarely eat meat because I don't want her to know that the look of disgust on my face is because my peripheral vision has caught her husband sucking ketchup out of his beard.

"I'm so sorry. I can have them remake it."

"No, I'll eat it, but it's massacred."

"I'm so sorry, I can have them remake it."

"So my fries can get cold?"

Her ass makes a sad face at the thought of the French fries leaving the table.

"I can bring you new fries. I'm so sorry, I can have them remake it."

"No, I'll eat it. But look at it! This is not medium rare!!"

"I'm so sorry, I can have them make remake it."

"No, I'll eat it, but it's not cooked right."

Yes, this has been established. You have two choices: Eat it or let me get you another one. All I can do is touch the "rare" key on the computer and hope the kitchen makes it correctly. Eat it or let me get you another one. She decides to eat it. And eat it she does. Every last bit of burger and fries is gone from both her plate and her husband's, although I am not certain he ate all of his. It is quite possible that a good deal of it was lost in that Bermuda Triangle he calls a beard. I swear to God I see a pickle in there, and we don't even serve pickles.

They do not want dessert, so I give them their check.

"Have a good night," I tell them. "I'll pick that up whenever you're ready."

"Well, I wish my burger would have been medium rare."

Again with this?

"I'm so sorry. I could have had them make remake it. I told you that."

"No, it's okay, I just wanted you to know."

Like I didn't already know. Everyone knows. She made sure that I knew and that the tables next to her knew, and she'll probably go home and write a review about it, too.

Do not complain for the sake of complaining. If you don't want me to fix the problem, then there is no need to tell me over and over again. I want to solve the problem. It will only make my tip better if you leave happy, but if you don't want me to resolve the issue, then your continual complaining is serving no purpose. Stop it.

The couple finally departs, leaving their table looking like a bomb exploded, with crumbs and burger juices all over the tabletop, chair, and floor. I pick up the cash and count the tip, surprised to see it is slightly more than 20 percent. You never can tell what you're going to get. Sometimes nice people leave you crap tips, and sometimes annoying people with big asses and blind husbands leave you good ones. What a world, what a world.

LESSON #8: *Don't be a douche bag.*

Dear D-bag Who Sat at Table 28 Last Night,

I just wanted to thank you for perpetuating the stereotype that men who go see stand-up comedy shows are gloober-globbery immature assholes who have no manners. I was wondering if that myth was a reality, and now I know it is true. It was so cool of you to walk into the club and immediately bellow out through your bloated face, "So do I buy my two drinks now or later?" We servers love to be yelled at. I loved how you said later as if there were an ah rather than an er at the end of the word. That was neat. I apologize that none of us thought it was as funny as you seemed to think it was. Thank you for understanding when we explained to you that it was table service only.

Kudos to you for finding such a sweet girlfriend. She seemed nice despite the way she kept her eyes pointed down at the floor every time you said something too loudly. At first glance, it seemed as if maybe she was embarrassed by you, but she was probably just looking down at the floor to see how clean it was, right? I mean, how could you ever embarrass her when you are wearing your pants so baggy that they hang past your ass? Wearing pants that way makes you cool, right? Yeah, I thought so.

When I took your order, I must admit I was surprised by what you wanted. I fully expected you to ask for a Long Island Iced Tea or a shot of Jägermeister®. But you just said "bottled water" in that cute way you have, dropping the r and adding an ah sound. Remember how I asked you if you wanted sparkling or flat, and you just said, "I dunno, just regular water!"

Manners matter! Always say "please" and "thank you."

That was adorable. Your girlfriend ordered a beer and then another beer, and I can only assume that it was to dull her senses and make sitting across from you more tolerable.

You know what else I loved about you, douche bag? I loved how you pulled your chair out from the table and then spread your legs apart really wide, presumably to give your huge package room to breathe. Never mind that it made it nearly impossible for me to walk past you every time I needed to get to Table 35. I'm sure your "boys" appreciated the fresh air.

Finally, douche bag: I am sorry I wasn't able to get to you as soon as you yelled "Wait-ah" across the room. I know you said it three or four times while waving your money at me. I heard you. I was just dealing with another table, and there were about twelve people between you and me at that moment. I couldn't get to you any sooner. Believe me, I really wanted to drop what I was doing, but sadly I was assisting another friendly, polite, and charming guest.

I look forward to seeing you again soon. Thank you for coming in and making my night so special. Most of all, thank you for the tip. I was very exited to hear that I could "keep the change" from the $60 that you gave me to cover your $55.14 check. It was the icing on the big, smelly, vinegar-and-water cake.

Mustard and mayo,

The Bitchy Waiter

P.S. I'm sorry I didn't have a plastic bag for you to carry your second bottled water. We don't normally have to-go bags, since we are a cocktail bar. Lucky for you, your girlfriend offered to put it in her purse. I know how difficult it would have been for you to carry a bottle in your own two hands, seeing how occupied they were with scratching your crotch.

LESSON #9: *Extra work deserves an extra tip.*

Maybe I'm wrong, but I believe that extra service deserves an extra tip. If customers ask me for extra everything, and I willingly and obediently comply with all their requests, shouldn't I be rewarded for that extra service that was given? Why, yes. Yes I should.

Two guys come in and sit at Table 15. They look like the kind of guys who would belong to a frat house called Kappa Sigma Douche Bag. One of them is wearing a hoodie emblazoned with an image of the #7 New York City subway train. When I see it, I wonder two things: Where would anyone *buy* something like that, and why would anyone *wear* something like that? The other guy has a short, thick neck that makes it look as if his earlobes are attached directly to his shoulders. My waist is most definitely smaller than the circumference of his neck, and I am fairly certain that if he were to use my belt for autoerotic asphyxiation, it would be way too small.

As soon as they sit down, they know what they want to drink. "Yo, can we get two margaritas on the rocks with extra salt?"

I tell the bartender about the extra salt request and go back to take their order.

No-Neck tries to turn his head in my direction but, finding it too difficult, decides to rotate his whole body toward me so he can speak. "I want a hamburger extra well done with extra cheddar and extra onions."

The subway aficionado growls out his order as well. "Gimme a cheeseburger, too. Well done. Extra cheese and extra pickles. And we want to start with two orders of the fried shrimp with extra sauce."

I place their order and go to pick up their margaritas at the bar. Tony has done an exceptional job of rimming the glasses with salt, and I feel certain that Mr. and Mr. Frat Boy will be pleased with the amount.

"Is that enough salt for you?" I ask. No-Neck casts his eyes down at the glass and attempts to shrug with indifference. The other one says, "It's all right. It'll do." In my mind, there is enough salt on the glass to satisfy the neediest of cattle hanging out at a salt lick, but these guys aren't your typical cattle, I guess.

They drink the margaritas in a matter of minutes, the straws making that slurping sound they do when there is nothing but ice left in the glass. I bring them their fried shrimp with extra sauce, let them know their burgers will be up in a few more minutes, and ask if they'd like another round of drinks. Of course, they do.

"Can you make sure they put extra salt on them this time?" As if it hadn't been done for the first round . . .

"Absolutely," I say through gritted teeth as I make my way to the bar. "Tony, these guys want extra salt, and they mean it. Go to town on these glasses, all right? Seriously, I want them to wake up tonight and feel like their tongues are wearing sweaters."

Tony picks up two glasses and puts all his focus on the rims. I watch him slice a lime in half and then coat the glass with the juice. He dips the glasses into the salt container and they come out saltier than the Dead Sea. "This ought to do it," he says.

For every ridiculous request, please tack an additional 1% onto the gratuity.

At this point, their burgers are in the window, so I take them the food while Tony finishes the drinks. As I place the burgers on the table, one asks for extra ketchup, and I assume that the other will want some as well, so I go to get two more ramekins of ketchup.

"Can I get some mayo?" one of them asks. "And I wanted extra onions, too," he adds, ignoring the extra onions already on his plate. I look at No-Neck, who is already cramming French fries into his eating hole, to see if he needs anything else. When I return with the mayo and onions, No-Neck says he, too, now wants mayo, and he also wants some extra napkins. I go to get the mayo and napkins, and I pick up the drinks on the way. Returning with everything they need, I realize they have asked for extra salt, extra pickles, extra sauce, extra onions, extra ketchup, extra mayo, and extra napkins. I proudly set down the margaritas, waiting to be thanked for the extraordinary amount of salt that is clinging to the sides of the glasses, but they simply ask for extra limes.

I wonder what they will tip me, and I feel that with all the extra requests and the extra trips I have made to their table, 20 percent should be a given. Their check is $100.13—even boys with heads as thick as tree stumps should be able to figure out 20 percent of that total. The amount of cash they leave cash on the table? $113. All that extra everything, and they can barely come up with a 12 percent tip. Maybe I'm wrong, but I believe all that extra service merits *at least* six Andrew Jacksons.

LESSON #10: *Just stop sitting at the dirty table.*

Can we talk about customers and their insane need to sit at the one dirty table in the whole fucking restaurant? It happened a few days ago to me, and I cannot wrap my tequila-soaked brain around it. The restaurant has three booths, all right next to one another. They are each the same in dimension, appearance, and distance from each other. I can see no discernible difference between any of them. Two of them are clean, with silverware and glasses, while one has a dirty plate on it, two glasses with water in them, and a couple of crumpled-up napkins. Two customers have just left the booth as another couple walked into the restaurant.

We don't have a hostess, so I greet them at the front and tell them to sit wherever they'd like. Like fucking moths to a flame or me to a margarita, they make a beeline for the one dirty booth and sit down. Why, God in heaven? Why do they do that? They actually walk past one clean booth to sit at the dirty one. I do not understand it. Menus in hand, I approach the table.

> **WHAT I SAY:** *"Hello, there. Give me a minute or two, and I will clean this table for you."*
>
> **WHAT I THINK:** *"Dumb asses. I hate you. I hate you so hard."*

Suddenly, they pull their heads out of their asses. "Oh, gosh. I didn't even notice this table is dirty. Do you want us to move?"

> **WHAT I SAY:** *"No, it's fine. I'll clean it right now. Don't worry about it."*
>
> **WHAT I THINK:** *"You didn't notice a pile of dirty fucking napkins sitting in front of you? And you didn't see that dessert plate with chocolate syrup all over it? You suck at seating yourself, and I hate you."*

Do people do this on purpose? Is there some deep, subconscious urge to take advantage of having a person serve them, so they do everything possible to have us do as much work for them as possible—including cleaning a table as they sit at it? Did they want to watch me scrub chocolate syrup off the table and get down on my knees before them to pick up the straw wrapper? As I am wiping the table down, a few errant bread crumbs make their way from my towel to the booth seat. I notice that the woman sees these crumbs, but I decide that the crumbs shall remain where they are. Had her ass not been sitting there, I would have wiped the booth seat down, too, but since she so desperately and immediately wanted this booth, the crumbs can sit with her.

"Okay, here are your menus, and I will be right back with place settings and glasses."

"Ummm, now the table is all wet," says the woman.

WHAT I SAY: *"Oh, gosh, I'm sorry. Let me get a dry cloth real quick and dry that off."*

WHAT I THINK: *"It's water, lady—get over it! Are your elbows going to dissolve if they touch moisture? It will be dry in thirty seconds. Good lord, you could have sat at the other, identical booth right behind you, and all would have been fine. But nooo, you needed to sit here and stare at another diner's mess, and then watch your lowly server wipe it clean for your Royal Shitty Highness. I haven't even begun my steps of service, and I am already seriously annoyed by you."*

I dry the table, take their order, and serve their food. Everything proceeds smoothly from then on, but I still can't help but wonder what in *tarnation* makes anyone want to sit at the one dirty table in a restaurant. Stop doing that, people. Really. Stop it.

THE ONLY THING DIRTIER THAN THE TABLE YOU JUST SAT DOWN AT IS MY APRON.

The Softer Side of Bitch

CIGARETTE LADY AT BOOTH 21

One of the worst things about waiting tables may be the people who sit in your station, but oddly enough, they can sometimes be one of the best things. I once served an amazingly cool lady who reminded me that being a waiter can be very rewarding. She is an older woman, all decked out in attire that was totally in style when she bought it thirty years ago. She is with a younger couple, and it seems as if they are taking Grandma out for dinner. When I tell her that the special of the night is gnocchi, her eyes light up. Suddenly very animated, she exclaims, "I love gnocchi! That's what I want."

Her voice is deep and gravelly, as if Lauren Bacall and Harvey Fierstein had a love child. It sounds like she doesn't just smoke cigarettes, but gargles with them as well. Like if she blew her nose, it might spew ashes.

"I grew up eating gnocchi," she says, "so I know what good gnocchi is like. I hope this passes the muster."

I look over at the open kitchen and smile at the Mexican cook who would be making it.

"Is it good?" she wants to know.

"Well, I like it a lot, but I didn't grow up eating it," I say. "Hopefully ours can compare to the memory of what you had, but if it doesn't, I can promise you that I will serve it with a smile."

She laughs at that, and then the laugh turns into a disturbing and violent cough that ends up with her grabbing a napkin and spitting into it. *"Good-bye, piece of lung,"* I think.

Fifteen minutes later, I place the bowl of gnocchi before her.

"Is there anything else I can get for you right now?"

She shakes her head as she grabs a utensil and focuses on the food in front of her.

"I'll be back in a few minutes and double-check on everything."

Already, she has her first bite on the fork and is blowing on it to cool it down. I stand across the dining room and watch her taste the gnocchi. She pops it into her mouth and her eyes move toward the ceiling and into the back of her head. It's usually a good sign when people roll their eyes into their skulls after taking a bite. Occasionally it means I forgot to tell the kitchen about their peanut allergy, but most of the time it means they are *loving* the taste of the food. It is time for my two-minute check-in.

"How do you like your gnocchi? Is it everything you want it to be and more?" I ask.

She takes a look at me and in her gravelly Eileen Heckart voice she says, "My dear, it is perfection. You made my night. Thank you."

She places her hand on my wrist and gives it a squeeze, and her smile reveals yellow teeth and nicotine-stained gums. I smile back at her.

"Good. I'm glad you like it. Enjoy your meal and let me know if there's anything else you need."

Sometimes waiting tables can give you varicose veins, a sore back, and fallen arches, but every once in a while it gives you a gift. This night it feels good to give this woman something to smile about. Clearly she is already a happy woman out for dinner with her family, but somehow I feel responsible for the smile on her face tonight. When I clear her plate, it is completely wiped clean.

"I think you really liked it, huh?"

"I loved it! Thank you so much, and please tell the chef how wonderful it was."

(*Como se dice "Cigarette Lady loved your gnocchi" en español?*)

"And you were a delight as well," she tells me.

She doesn't care for dessert or coffee because she says she doesn't need anything else after such a perfect meal. They pay the check and leave after one more brief coughing spell. As I wipe the table, I feel this weird sense of satisfaction that I don't get often enough at my job. The woman had a wonderful time in my station, and she was completely fulfilled by the food and the experience. Thank you, Cigarette Lady. You reminded me that servers have the ability to create new, positive memories or bring back old memories for their guests, and, in your case, I think I did both. I imagine that as she crawls into bed with her pack of cigarettes and thinks about her day, she might think of me and the plate of gnocchi I gave to her.

CHAPTER THREE

I HATE YOUR KIDS

IT'S NOT EASY FOR A PERSON TO ADMIT THAT HE doesn't like children. It's practically taboo to admit that you find children as endearing as a case of herpes, but I challenge anyone to wait tables for a few months and not at least consider the notion. Dealing with the children of parents who don't care that their child is coloring on the wall and throwing chicken nuggets across the room is enough to make anyone dislike kids. Sure, we all know that we should hate the parent and not the child, but in my world I find it much more satisfying to say, "I hate your fucking baby."

Rice Tragedy at Table 16

There is a minor trend sweeping across the United States: Restaurants are banning children. Of course, restaurant owners have the right to serve whomever they please, but the ban is not sitting well with parents. In discussing the subject, there are good points made on both sides of the argument. I was almost convinced that maybe a restaurant didn't have the right to ban children, but then a couple showed up in my station with their two-year-old son. Thank you, couple, for reminding me why I bow down to the wisdom of any restaurant owner/manager who says, "Take your kid and shove it up your ass."

The lovely young family is very friendly and polite. Without any hesitation, they order a glass of wine, a beer, some calamari, and two roasted chicken breasts. They do not order for their son. I assume they are going to let him eat off their plates. *I wish.* As soon as I drop off the chicken, they ask for their check because they say they don't know how long the kid is going to remain so calm. "I totally understand," I say. As I print their check, I think about how conscientious they are being. They want to be able to make a quick getaway if he starts to act a fool, and I really appreciate it. They gobble down their chicken and bolt out surprisingly fast. I thank them as they breeze past me at the bar and I head back to clear their table. What is waiting for me is a shocking mess.

I thought the parents were both humans, but I now realize they must have been made of grain, for they produced a child made of white rice. There are piles of rice all over the place, and I didn't even serve them rice. Is rice the new cereal—the one item that parents won't leave home without so children can have both sustenance and something to throw all over the floor? There is enough rice on the floor to make a dozen California rolls. It looks like a rice ball has exploded. Or maybe a rice and bean burrito (hold the beans) had thrown up. When I was kid, I went to the Houston Zoo and saw a monkey taking his own crap and throwing it all over the place. Was this kid pooping out rice and doing his best chimpanzee impersonation? There is rice everywhere—on the table, in the booth,

on the sides of the booth, on the floor, and under the table next to the booth. There is probably some on the ceiling, but I refuse to let myself look up because then I would be responsible for cleaning it. No wonder they left the restaurant so quickly. They were ashamed of the Rice Terror that decimated Table 16.

I go to get the broom and dustpan and start sweeping it all up. Have you ever tried to sweep up cooked rice? It doesn't sweep. It sticks to the floor and the broom and just moves from one spot to another, refusing to go into the dustpan. The table next to Rice Abomination gives me a look that says one of two things: "I'm sorry you have to clean up after that messy kid" or "I'm sorry about your whole life-choice situation." One of the women at the sympathetic booth is very pregnant, and it is hard for me to resist telling her something like, "You'd better not become one of these kind of hateful parents who let their kids do whatever they fucking want in a restaurant." (When Preggo orders her hamburger, she makes sure to tell me three times that it needs to be very well done because she is pregnant, as if I can't tell. I think elephants gestate for less time than this woman. Her baby's arm is practically hanging out of her vagina trying to grab a French fry.)

Mr. and Mrs. Rice Crop have a check that is $63.00 and they leave me a $12 tip, which is right at 20 percent. However, when I have to get on my knees under a table with a roll of paper towels, I expect more than 20 percent, people. My knees are weak, and it takes a lot of effort to get on them. Cleaning up enough rice to feed a family of four deserves at least a 25 percent tip and also a "Really sorry about the mess" acknowledgment. So, banning children under the age of six from restaurants? Bring it on.

Waffles for Beelzebub

I know the three-year-old kid at Table 8 is trouble the moment he rolls into the restaurant in his fancy stroller. His shifty eyes give him away, and I can tell that he has plans to ruin my night. He shoots me a crusty look with his big, blue eyes, and I shoot him one right back with my bloodshot ones. We already have an understanding: "I don't like you, and you don't like me."

"Mark my words," I say to the bartender. "That asshole baby is going to knock over his glass of water, I guarantee it."

The bartender ignores me because he is tired of hearing about my possibly imagined personal vendettas with every toddler who lands in my station.

I greet the table and see that the kid already has a small baggie of cereal in front of him. With pure deliberation, he reaches into the bag and retrieves one solitary morsel. He makes eye contact with me, and I watch him drop the multigrain goodness onto the floor.

"I want chocolate milk," he tells his mother.

"We don't have chocolate milk," I inform her. I grin slightly and shift my eyes to the little boy.

"How about regular milk?" I suggest, knowing that regular is a poor substitute for chocolate.

"Just water for him, thanks," Mom says.

I return with a small plastic cup half full of water and place it before the child.

"Be careful, sweetie. Don't spill it," the mother tells her son.

He pulls the cup closer to his chest while looking at me with narrowed eyes. The left side of his upper lip curls into a devilish smile. We both know it is only a matter of time before the water spills, and I am cleaning it up.

I am reciting the dinner specials when the little boy informs his mother that he will be having waffles. It's dinnertime, and we don't even have waffles on Sunday brunch, but this kid thinks he's gonna get a waffle out of me? I wouldn't find a waffle for this brat for any reason in the world. He can go home and have a frozen one, but not on my watch, and not in my station.

"Sweetie, they don't have waffles. How about a burger?"

"Waffles."

"How about pasta?"

"Waffles!"

"How about a peanut butter and jelly sandwich?"

"We don't have peanut butter and jelly sandwiches," I interrupt.

"WAFFLES!!" screams the boy while throwing his hands up in disgust and anguish, consequently knocking over the cup of water.

Instinctively, I pull the bar towel from my apron and catch the water before it drips onto the mother's lap. Out of the corner of my eye, I see the little devil cross his arms with smug satisfaction, and I look at the bartender to make sure he sees that my prediction has come true. He seems not to care that I am in my personal hell with a three-year-old child.

"I'm so sorry," says the mother. "That was an accident."

Two of us know it was no accident.

"Waffles," he says again, this time with a hint of self-satisfaction.

The mother decides that she will order him the closest thing that we have to waffles, which is our special of the day, zucchini pancakes. I don't

IF YOUR BABY IS DOING THIS,

PLEASE LEAVE THE
RESTAURANT.

know what world she is living in to think that a kid is going to be satisfied with sautéed shredded vegetables as a substitute for waffle deliciousness. The toddler looks at me as if he has won the game. He thinks he beat me because he's getting pancakes after I told him we don't have waffles. I eagerly ring in the order, looking forward to the disappointment that is sure to come, and put a rush on it.

Six minutes later, I am back at the table with a plate of zucchini pancakes that have a big dollop of sour cream on top of them. I place it in front of the little boy. "Here you go! Pancakes just for you. Yummy, yummy, yummy!"

His eyes focus on the sour cream. "Is that ice cream?" he asks with excitement. I back away to see how the question will be answered.

"Well, it's not *really* ice cream, but it is *sour* cream," says the mom with an air of desperation. "I guess it's *sorta* like ice cream, wouldn't you say so?" she asks me.

I stare into the little boy's face and, with fierce conviction, say, "It's *totally* like ice cream. I can hardly tell the difference."

I am about to watch this kid take a huge bite of zucchini pancakes with sour cream when he is expecting regular pancakes with ice cream, and I am trembling with excitement to see how supremely pissed off he is going to be. His mother puts a big bite of nonwaffle onto the fork and zooms it toward his mouth. Inside it goes, and I see the realization dawning over the face of the child. His eyes show his revulsion, and I can tell that he is about to spit it out and throw a fit, but then he looks at me with eyes of steely reserve. It's as if he does not want to give me the satisfaction of knowing that he hates his dinner. He knows that if he spits it out, I win. Slowly and with great difficulty, he swallows the zucchini and sour cream.

"You like it?" asks the mother. "You like those pancakes?"

"Yeah, how's that ice cream?" I ask. "You like that ice cream? I'm gonna go get you some more!"

I retrieve a ramekin full of sour cream and dump it onto his plate. His mother continues to feed him the pancake that I know he hates, and he continues to eat it in order to prove that he is right. In my mind, the game is over and I am the victor.

Twenty-five minutes later, they are gone. I go to the table to clear it off and underneath the booth I see a pile of cereal—not just a little, but a whole baggie's worth. It has been ground into a fine powder that is going to require me to get on my knees and sweep. Maybe I didn't win the epic battle between us because he is gone and I am still here cleaning up after him. Knowing that he ate a whole plate of nasty-ass zucchini pancakes when he wanted waffles makes the cleaning easier, but I must admit he was a good challenger. Maybe I am not the victor after all, but neither is he. Perhaps it is a draw.

The battle is not over, kid. I will win the next time. I guarantee it.

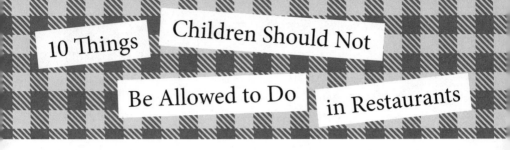

10 Things Children Should Not Be Allowed to Do in Restaurants

1. **THEY SHOULD NEVER LEAVE CEREAL ALL OVER THE DAMN PLACE,** because I don't want to sweep that up.

2. **THEY SHOULD NEVER TRY TO ORDER FOR THEMSELVES** when they can't read a menu and they don't like to talk to strangers, because I am in a hurry and don't have time for that.

3. **THEY SHOULD NEVER SPILL THEIR DRINK** after they refuse to accept a cup with a lid on it, because I will scream, "I told you this would happen!"

4. **THEY SHOULD NEVER LEAVE THEIR DIRTY DIAPERS** anyplace other than the trash can, because it lets the world know they have awful parents.

5. **THEY SHOULD NEVER JUST SIT THERE IN THEIR STROLLER** like they own the place, because I don't want to be judged by a two-year-old.

6. **THEY SHOULD NEVER REQUIRE ME TO DO EXTRA WORK,** like walk all the way to the back of the restaurant to get a high chair or a booster seat, because it means I will then have to wipe down that high chair or booster seat, and I'm not in the mood.

7. **THEY SHOULD NEVER PROMISE THEY WILL ONLY USE THE CRAYONS ON THE PAPER,** because as soon as I turn around they will break that promise and use them on the wall.

8. **THEY SHOULD NEVER SCREAM AT THE TOP OF THEIR LUNGS,** because it makes it impossible for me to concentrate on really important things, like making coffee and rolling silverware.

9. **THEY SHOULD NEVER RUN ALL OVER THE RESTAURANT,** because you never know what they might run into or what I might drop on them by "total and complete accident."

10. **THEY SHOULD NEVER SMILE IN THE SWEETEST WAY** or say something really cute, because it makes me feel like an asshole for saying how much I dislike children.

The Good Ship, Butter Packet

...the story of an adorable little girl who is sitting in my station. With her head of blond curls and pudgy little cheeks, she looks just like everyone's favorite singing toddler, Shirley Temple. Well, this little girl looks like Shirley Temple if she had just eaten Laurel and Hardy. She is Shirley Temple, the large economy size.

With the assistance of her parents, she slides into the booth and immediately faces the other direction, hanging her cute little sausage arms over her booth and into the booth behind her. She is now effectively part of another couple's dining experience.

"Hi," she says to the man and woman who are trying to enjoy their meal sans Moppet Head. So cute. I love when the kid in the booth behind me wants to talk to me, don't you?

I go to greet the family. I expect that Shirley Temple will jump onto the table and do a tap-dance number with Buddy Ebsen, but instead she sits politely in her seat and listens as I explain the specials. She is not interested in the sautéed shrimp with garlic or the herbed chicken and vegetable soup—and certainly *not* the pork medallions with collard greens. None of these things are to her liking. No, this little girl has other food in mind.

"I want pasta!" She beams, pointing at herself with her thumb in such a way that the curls on her head bounce. "And mashed potatoes, too. Yummy!"

She rubs her belly and laughs. I wonder if she'd like an appetizer of animal crackers. I make eye contact with her mother to see if she approves of her daughter's high-carb order, and the mother seems satisfied. Who am I to judge? If the little girl wants pasta and potatoes, so be it. Who needs vegetables? Not this little girl.

I place the order and go on with my other customers. As I pass by the little girl's table, her father asks me a question.

"Do you have any bread?"

"Of course. I'll be right back."

Two minutes later, I place the bread in the center of the table. The father picks it up and hands the entire basket to his daughter.

"Here you go, sweetie. Here's your bread and butter."

I watch the family to see if anyone other than Shirley Temple eats any bread. They don't. It is so cute when she picks up that half a loaf of bread with her cute little ham hock hands and shoves it into her mouth. I tell the chef that we need her pasta and mashed potatoes as soon as possible, seeing that this little girl is clearly on her way to starvation. Within five minutes, Carbohydrate Dinner is ready.

"Can I has some ketchup, please?" Again she points at herself with her thumb.

I get the ketchup for her and watch as she dumps it on top of her penne. I have a feeling that tomato ketchup is as close as she is going to get to a fruit or vegetable serving. She cleans both plates, and her parents congratulate her on doing such a "big girl job" with her dinner, the key words being *big* and *girl*.

She asks for dessert and her parents refuse, so she gives a cute little pout and puts her hands on her hips. Then she picks up two butter packets, opens them, and licks them clean. Nothing is cuter than watching a little girl eat butter.

Her kind parents leave me a 20 percent tip. The father helps his daughter put her shoes back on—they had fallen off her feet at some point during the meal, possibly because her little piggies were crying out for relief. They help her off the bench and put her coat on.

"Good night, everybody!" says Super-Size Shirley. "Thanks for everything!"

She glances back at the table to make sure there are no butter packets left for eating and skips out the door, her hair bouncing all around like little curly fries.

Grabby McGrab Grab Baby

It's no news in this old court that babies are not my favorite things. Sure, they're cute, and people say they smell good, but who hasn't seen at least one baby who was clearly hit in the head with an ugly stick? As my seventh-grade teacher Mr. Trowbridge would say, when encountering a less than attractive bundle of joy, "Now, *that's* a baby!" And speaking as one who took care of a baby for a full year, there are plenty of times when they most assuredly and most definitely do not smell anywhere close to good. If "good" was in one neighborhood, you would need to take the G train and two buses to get to the neighborhood she smelled like after a lunch of chicken nuggets and kimchi. Don't get me wrong, though. I loved that baby I took care of. Still do. But sometimes she was *stanky*. There is a baby at Table 11, and before you say that I should hate the parents and not the baby, I know that already. It's just that I take every opportunity I can to say, "I hate babies."

The first indication that this baby and I would be having issues is when the high chair goes at the end of the table, and now the baby is right in front of the sidestand. Anytime I need to get a spoon, I have to reach right behind the baby. What is wrong with this baby? Doesn't she know she is in my way? Why are babies so unaware of their spatial relationship to other people and things? Man, babies are so clueless. Every time I approach the table, that baby reaches out to touch my hair. Granted, my hair is amazing, and the baby isn't the only one in the restaurant who wants to touch it. I let the lady at Booth 7 touch my hair because she complimented me so highly, and I liked her Louisiana accent. I also figure it will help me get a bigger tip. The baby, however, has no accent at all, and her hands are probably sticky with jelly, lollipop, or poop. And babies are notoriously bad tippers. Man, babies can't do anything.

Halfway through the meal, the baby knocks over a glass of water. It spills all over the table and onto the mom and then onto the floor. Why did I bother giving the baby a plastic cup with a lid if she was determined to use a full-sized glass of water, anyway? Man, babies have shitty motor skills. The mom doesn't get up, even though water has just been poured all over her lap. She doesn't even flinch. She must be used to her baby always spilling crap all over her. As I am trying to clean it up, she doesn't budge. I get down on my hands and knees with some paper towels and soak up as much water as I can, while she is too unconcerned to even move her chair over two inches. Meanwhile, the baby grabs a handful of my locks and won't let go. "Oh, look, she likes your hair," says Lazy Mom. I smile and think about how *everyone* likes my hair. It doesn't make your baby a child genius or anything—get over it. When it becomes clear that this spill is as cleaned up as it is going to get, I give up. I will let the hardwood floors do the rest of the work for me. Soak it up, hardwood. I do not bring them another glass of water because that greedy baby will probably

Misbehaving children will not be tolerated.

just grab it and toss it to the floor in another attempt to get at my precious locks. Not gonna fall for that one, baby.

They give me a good tip, and the baby waves at me as they leave the restaurant. On second glance, the baby is kinda cute, with her little stubby fingers and her hair pulled into a barely there ponytail. On the table is a red crayon that has rolled underneath the plate. I pick it up and run out to the sidewalk to catch them. "You left something on your table your baby might want." The baby reaches out to grab the crayon, and the mother says, "Thank you." "Bye-bye, baby," I say. "Have a good night." She coos out something that I can't completely understand, but it sounds like "You have amazing hair."

Stroller Bitches from Hell

This is a rant about the Upper East Side women, their massive strollers, and their even more massive whorelike attitudes. And this time, I have photographic evidence of these mythical creatures that seek me out to torture me with too many questions and far too many special dietary needs. They roll in and sit on the patio right under the sign that says, PLEASE SEE HOSTESS INSIDE RESTAURANT FOR SEATING.

Although I watch them sit down, I wait until one comes inside to ask for a menu before I acknowledge their presence. One lady has a double stroller, while the other lady has a single stroller. They both, however, have Resting Bitch Face Syndrome. The strollers are taking up a ridiculous amount of space. The lady with the double-wide has so much crap inside the stroller that I cannot even be certain there are actual babies inside it. All I see are about fifty blankets, a dozen pillows, and a ton of stuffed animals. Occasionally, I hear a muffled cry. I can't be sure what the cry is about, but I imagine the baby is trying to say that she hates her mother and can't wait to learn to talk, so she can tell her so. The moms barricade themselves behind the table, making it impossible for me to get within two feet of them. Every time I need to serve them something, I am forced to pass it to them over the strollers. They look irritated about that, and that makes me happy. I hand them the waters (which I never refill) and then hand them their salads (which have plenty of substitutions and things on the side). I never clear the table because I honestly cannot get to it. The size of these fucking strollers! Is it really necessary for them to be this large? These children don't live in the strollers, do they? Please tell me that I am not looking at their bedrooms-on-wheels.

They never say "thank you" or even look at me. I go out to the patio two times to see if they are ready to pay, but the check sits in the lap of Bitch Face #1. Later, I look out the window to see her holding the check up in the air with her back to me. There she is, waving the check as if to say, "I am ready for you to take care of my needs. I am Queen of all

Stroller Moms, and I will mow you over with my Titanic Stroller of Death if you don't attend to me immediately."

When they finally leave, their table is a wreck. On it are four jars of baby food and a pile of baby wipes that are covered in something that better have been mashed peas. As they roll away, I curse them under my breath and feel sorry for the babies, who will no doubt grow up to be just as entitled as their giant-stroller-wielding mothers.

My stroller is bigger than many New York City apartments.

DO NOT TOUCH BABY

The Baby Speaks

Hi, peoples,

I'm that fourteen-month-old baby who sat in your station last night. I didn't feel like napping this morning, so I crawled my diaper-wearing ass over to my mom's laptop to kill some time fucking up my mommy's winning streak on that online word game. (Sorry, Mommy, but I just played "CAT" and left the triple-word score open, where your sister can now play "AXED," with the X getting the triple word two times. I know it's mean of me, but that's what you get for giving me a bite of apple last night when it should have been abundantly clear that I was screaming for a fucking cookie.) Anyway, my mom left her computer open to a page called "The Bitchy Waiter," and I started reading it, and I have one to thing to say about this "Bitchy Waiter" person: What an asshole.

First off, I don't even know why my mommy would be reading this blog. She's not a waitress. (Note to self: Remind Mommy that I want my apple-sauce served in a bowl next time, and not a coffee cup, and tell her she needs to wash her apron. It's filthy with food stains, cat hair, and baby vomit.) After reading a few months' worth of blog posts from this guy, it seems as if he has something against me. Being a baby, I had to respond.

Yes, I make a mess when I go to a restaurant—get over it. I barely have any motor skills to begin with, but you're gonna flip your shit just because I spill a few Cheerios® on the floor? It's your job to sweep that floor, anyway, so what's the big deal? What do you want me to do, get a broom and sweep it up myself? I'm still trying to understand this whole potty training thing, and you expect me to handle a broom? Not gonna happen. Besides, I don't even want the Cheerios. I have been begging for Cap'n Crunch® for like six months now, but every time we leave the house, Mommy makes sure we have an enormous baggie filled with Cheerios. I keep thinking that if I just throw them on the floor, she will get that I don't like them. Sorry that creates more work for you. Cry me a fucking river, waiter. And go get me some damn crayons.

**Looks can be deceiving.
I'm an asshole.**

Another thing: Stop holding big, heavy trays right over my head. Uh, hello? My skull is not fully formed yet, and if you drop a skillet of fajitas on it, you could do some serious damage. Not to mention, it might stain my new onesie that I got as a gift from some lady who works with my daddy. Wouldn't it make more sense to serve food around me? Okay, I just realized that most of the time my mommy and daddy place me at the head of the table and in the aisle, so I guess that would make it difficult for you. I will talk to them about that, and when I say "talk to them," I mean "cry," and usually when I cry they just give me a bottle, so I don't really expect there to be any change any time soon.

And about that time my diaper was changed in a booth? I was totally against that. It was humiliating. I screamed and yelled and cried, and I even peed all over the booth in protest, but she kept right on replacing my dirty diaper in front of a couple of women sharing a Caesar salad like it was no big deal. Yes, I peed in the booth, and no, we didn't clean it up. Please, if my mommy can't be bothered to pick up a few Cheerios off the floor, do you really think she's going to mop up a puddle of urine? It's your job to mop anyway, right, waiter?

I also would like to discuss breast-feeding in a restaurant. If my mommy is going to eat at a table, then I want to eat at the table, too. I know that her lactating boobies are not the most fun thing for you to look at when you're trying to refill a water glass, but that's how it goes. Maybe you think it would be better for her to take me into the bathroom, but I really don't want to eat while she is sitting on the toilet. She does that at home way too often, and when I am out in a restaurant I want it to feel like it's a special occasion. Besides, the time that I have to suckle my mommy is limited, and I will not be able to do it forever. It is something I will probably only get to do for like five or six more years, and I want to take advantage of it as often as I can. So whether we are home watching Real Housewives, or on the Q32 bus, or in your station at the restaurant, I'm not gonna apologize for it.

Okay, I'd better wrap this up. My naptime will be over soon, and Mommy will be coming in here to check on me any minute—unless she had an extra glass of wine, in which case I have an extra half hour. In conclusion, I want to remind all you servers to chill the fuck out. You were babies once, too, you know. If you don't like us, then deal with our parents. They're the ones who make the decisions. Well, we make some decisions. For instance, I just now decided that I am going to take a dump as I type this last paragraph. I understand that I could crawl over to the bathroom *and sit on the My Little Poopy Pony toilet, but I'm gonna be a baby for as long as I can. The next time I go to a restaurant, I promise not to throw Cheerios onto the floor if you promise to stop rolling your eyes every time you see my stroller. Okay, my dump is finished. Hopefully, Mommy is done with her wine break because I'm gonna start crying now so she can come clean me up.*

Bye, bye, bitches.

I Hate Kids, #378

When the woman comes in with her three sons, I think nothing of the matter. The boys are aged seven to about twelve, and they seem reasonably well behaved, with two of them having some kind of mobile device that will keep them occupied while they wait for their meal. Five minutes later, another couple arrives with their two sons, and I make the decision to seat them next to the other table with children so that all of them can be contained in one section—much as I would do if I discovered that they all were carrying a rare strain of influenza. As we approach the booth, I hear one mother say to the other mother, "Well, look who's here! I didn't know you would be here. Boys, look who it is!"

Squeals of excitement erupt from the five boys. They are good friends, and they act as if they have not seen each other for months when, in all likelihood, they had probably just had lunch together not six hours earlier at their school cafeteria. Suddenly, the noise level in the back section of the restaurant increases several decibels, and I watch two tables merge together into a big eight-top of prepubescence.

"What is this, Chuck E. Cheese's?" asks the bartender as he hands me a tray of lemonades and sodas.

"I know. It's only going to get worse, I'm sure."

The parents make a minimal effort to keep the kids under control, but repeating the phrase "Remember what we told you" is not nearly as effective as half a nonprescription antihistamine tablet would be. The

AS GOD IS MY WITNESS, I'LL NEVER SERVE CHILDREN AGAIN!

boys move from table to table, and I no longer know who belongs to whom, nor do I care. When one child begins making monkey sounds, the other four quickly follow suit. One mom threatens to take away the lemonades, but the monkey sounds continue. I consider getting bananas from the kitchen and cramming them down their throats, but I can't find any, so I pick up the next best thing: a bar towel that was just used to clean under the ice machine. Deciding that it may be inappropriate for me to stuff dirty rags into the mouths of babes, I instead shoot them some dirty looks, which go largely unnoticed.

"Stop it!" yells one of the mothers.

The monkey sounds continue, and I watch as the mom pulls the lemonade away from the main little chimp asshole and puts it on the other side of the table.

"I told you I would take away your lemonade if you didn't behave," she says.

"But I didn't hear you say that," he responds.

Please, you disruptive little asswipe: You know you heard your mom say that. The whole restaurant heard her say that. There is probably an old man in New Jersey who had his hearing aid turned up high enough to hear it, because she screeched it to you at least five times, and it got louder each time she said it. After a whole two seconds of no more monkey sounds, she rewards him by giving back the lemonade. I look at the pile of dirty rags in the dish room and tell the dishwasher not to throw them away just yet.

The meal continues, as do the empty threats.

"Remember what we told you?"

"I will take away your lemonades again."

"Get up off the floor, or you're going to regret it."

Once they have all had dessert (these kids obviously need a little bit more sugar to liven things up!), the mothers talk as the kids run rampant, taking over the entire back section of the restaurant. I watch one boy repeatedly run to and from the restroom, laughing wildly each time.

"What's going on in there that's so funny?" I ask.

"Mouth farts!"

"I'm sorry, what?"

"Mouth farts! It's when you need to burp, so you go to the bathroom and do it in the toilet."

All of the kids are giggling. The parents are oblivious.

"Do what in the toilet?" I ask.

"You lean over the toilet and burp into it. That's called a mouth fart. Duh."

I laugh and think that it sounds like something my brothers and I would have done when we were kids if our parents would have let us run around restaurants completely unsupervised, which they didn't.

"Mouth farts, huh? Good to know, good to know," I say as I clear away some dirty dishes and paper towels.

Finally, the parents ask for their checks, and they push the tables back to where they had been. I watch them as they do a cursory sweep of the floor, picking up stray French fries and napkins and placing them on the one remaining empty plate still on the table. They each leave me a 20 percent tip, and the five boys run out ahead of their parents as each adult thanks me for putting up with them.

Future Douche Bag of America

At first glance, he appears to be your average thirteen-year-old boy—gawky, with a little bit of acne, and irritated by his mother, just like most boys his age. When he and his mother arrive at the restaurant, there is only one table available. Without waiting for me to lead the way, the boy makes a beeline for it, like he's a little old Asian lady getting onto the F train at the East Broadway stop, paying no mind to anyone who may be in his path. He throws himself onto the chair and exclaims that he does not need the menu. The mother agrees.

"How are you?" she asks me. The mother is a regular, and we often bump into each other at the grocery store and around the neighborhood. She's nice and I like her.

Before I can answer, the boy sighs heavily. "I'm starving," he whines.

"No you're not. You're hungry," corrects his mother.

"Gargh," says the boy, giving the impression that he is somehow clearing his throat sarcastically. He throws his sweater off his shoulders and onto his chair, letting his head fall back in utter disbelief that his mother is not going to get food for him right this very second.

After the mother and I are finished with our pleasantries, the boy says, "*Now* can we order? Gawd! I want the steak well done with the fries

Pointing at your watch and snapping your fingers do not make your server move faster.

on the side" (as opposed to the fries cooked inside the steak, I suppose). "And an order of calamari."

His mother places her order, using phrases that her son seems unaccustomed to, such as "please" and "thank you."

"Okay," I say. "I'll go put this order in and it will be out shortly." I return my pen to my apron and start to walk away when the boy decides he has one more thing to say.

"And that calamari? Put a rush on it!"

I look at the kid and he morphs before my very eyes. No longer is he the slightly annoying teenager in khaki pants and a blue button-down shirt, just discovering the joys of puberty. He now appears to me as a full-fledged douche bag–in–training. Suddenly, he resembles that asshole in every movie that took place in a high school during the 1980s, like Steff in *Pretty in Pink*.

I look at his mother, who shrugs her shoulders as if she has resigned herself to having a douche bag for a son.

"You got it," I say. "A rush on the calamari."

I mosey toward the computer, making sure to check on every other table first and fill any waters that need attention. Before I get to the computer, I see that the bread plates need to be restocked and that the napkins are low, so I take care of those tasks and then I help myself to a soda before I place the order for the calamari, conveniently forgetting to add the word *rush* to the ticket.

Ten minutes later, when I place the appetizer before Douche Bag, Jr., he reaches out to grab a handful and stuff it into his face. He doesn't give me time to warn him that it has just come out of the fryer and is very, very hot. It doesn't matter. The piping-hot calamari is no match for the fiery douchiness that his mouth is used to accommodating, and he swallows it with ease.

After their appetizer plates have been cleared, Douche Bag, Jr. wants to know how much longer it will be before his well-done steak is ready. I assure him it will be on his table as soon as it is ready, because the sooner it's ready, the sooner I can serve it, the sooner he can eat it, and the sooner his vinegar-and-water ass will be out of my section. My explanation is not good enough for him because moments later I see him stand up and walk over to our open kitchen to hover at the line, with his hands on his hips, watching his steak on the grill. A watched pot may never boil, but a steak being eyed by a thirteen-year-old douche bag cooks more quickly—everybody knows that.

"How much longer for the steak?" he asks Juan, the grill cook.

I intervene. "I will bring your steak as soon as it's finished. I promise. Go sit down."

The rest of their meal ensues without a hitch. The steak must have calmed his douchiness for now, but certainly not for the future. He has a lot to look forward to in life. When he gets to high school, he won't be joining Future Business Leaders of America or Future Farmers of America; he will start his own club called Future Douche Bags of America. He will be the president as well as the vice-president, and will rule with an iron fist. His shirt collar will always be in a popped position, his chin will always be thrust forward, and his attitude will always suck. Good luck, ladies—he's thirteen, and he's all yours.

The Softer Side of Bitch

SHERMAN DOESN'T LIVE HERE ANYMORE

t's Thursday, and I don't want to go to the restaurant today, and it's not for the usual reasons. Every Thursday, I go to work at 4:00, arriving before the other server and the bartender, so I can fill the ketchups, stock the paper towels, and leave at 10:00. Somewhere between 5:30 and 6:30, I begin to look out the window of the restaurant because I know that my husband, Mark, will be walking our dog, Sherman, down to say hello. It's our little Thursday tradition. The bartender and the other server know to look for them and watch my station while I go out and give my husband a kiss and Sherman a belly rub. It is by far my favorite thing about working at the restaurant on Thursdays. Today is different because they will not be making that walk. We had to say good-bye to Sherman two days ago.

Mark and I got Sherman on August 23, 1998, when he was just seven weeks old. From that day on, he was our number one priority. After fifteen years, we had to make the hardest decision we have ever had to make. It was a day we had dreaded since we first got him, and there was no way to prepare for it. Growing up in the country, it was not uncommon to discover one day that your dog was gone. Maybe he had been hit by a car, he'd gotten lost, or he'd been shot at by some angry farmer who was protecting his chickens. Sherman, though, lived in our apartment and shared every single moment with us.

Last Thursday—the day we made the decision—I texted Mark: "Make sure you boys walk down here today, all right?" Sherman was very old and didn't like to walk much, but I knew it would be the last time he paid the restaurant a visit. I was at a table on the patio when I saw them standing out in front, so I whisked by the bar, saying that I'd be right back. Sherman looked tired from his three-block journey. I bent down to scratch his head, and my eyes filled with tears as he pulled his head away from my hand and turned to walk back home. Mark was crying, too. We hugged and cried on the street as my tables probably wondered why the bartender was taking care of them now. "Good-bye, little baby dog. I'll see you in a few hours." Mark picked up Sherman and headed back to our apartment. I went back to Table 16 with red, swollen eyes and asked if they needed another glass of wine.

Two days have passed, and his water bowl is just where he left it. The fridge still has his food in it, his bed is still waiting for him, and I probably still have baggies in most of my pants pockets. Every time I am at work, I look for little things to get me through the shift. Maybe one of my customers will cheer me up by doing something that reminds me of Sherman: eat half their food and then decide it tastes horrible and leave the rest, or completely ignore me while I am talking to them. I know that around 5:30, I will instinctively begin to look out the window to see if my boys are there.

We will miss Sherman. And Thursdays at the restaurant will never be the same. Fast forward two years, and the tradition continues with our new dog Parker.

·~ঞ৶·

Return of the Douche

The benefit of working in the same restaurant for five years, as I have, is that I see the same customers repeatedly, and they become my regulars. The worst thing about working in the same restaurant for five years, as I have, is that I see the same customers repeatedly, and they become my regulars. At least two years have passed since my nostrils have been filled with acrid fumes from the Future Douche Bag of America, yet here he is today in all his glory. His mother has been in many times and I had almost forgotten that she produced this pile of waste she has for a son. He has grown since I last saw him; his upper lip sports a hint of peach fuzz and his forehead a virtual field of whiteheads that look like tiny little cauliflowers about to explode. His gangly legs are extended into the aisle, and his gigantic feet are in my way. I have to step over his bright white sneakers several times throughout the course of their meal.

"How are you guys tonight?" I ask mother and son.

"I need bread," he answers, forgetting that a demand for carbs is not the correct answer to being asked about your state of being.

"Please," scolds mom.

"Pleeeease," says the son as he releases his neck muscles in such a way that his head practically rests on his back.

I can tell that he is probably on his second or third term of serving as president of the Future Douche Bags of America. Within a couple of minutes, I return with the bread, and he promptly reaches into the basket to grab a piece, not allowing me to set it on the table. He cannot wait to have that yeasty goodness in his mouth, and I know it's only a matter of a few years before this douche bag will be dealing with a different kind of yeast, in the form of an infection that he picked up from a girl he convinced to sleep with him.

"We do have a special appetizer tonight of vegetarian spring rolls with a dipping sauce of—"

"Do they have shrimp in them?" he wants to know.

"No, they're vegetarian. There is no shrimp. They come with a dipping sauce of—"

"So, no shrimp?"

"No. No shrimp, just a dipping sauce of—"

"Bring me those."

"Please," his mother reminds him.

"Pleeeease," he says, this time with an Olympic-caliber eye roll.

He never does hear what the dipping sauce is, and for all he knows it's one made of recycled menus, bull semen, and castor oil. When the spring rolls are ready, I take them to the table and, just like last time with

MAKING EYE CONTACT WITH YOUR SERVER WILL USUALLY GET YOU BETTER SERVICE.

the calamari, he shoves the food into his mouth with no concern about the potential temperature of the spring rolls that had come out of a deep fryer only thirty seconds earlier.

"Were these fried in peanut oil?" he asks me, through a mouthful of fried rice paper, cabbage, and carrots. "Because I'm allergic to that."

I decide to take half a second longer than necessary to answer his question to see if he realizes that it doesn't really matter if they were fried in peanut oil or not, since he is already eating it. Unless he has an epinephrine autoinjector handy, he'd better hope the answer is no. He takes another bite before I let him know that he is safe from the evils of peanuts.

"Okay, good. That woulda been bad," he says.

"Would it have really been that bad?" I think. *"I'm not so sure."*

Mother and son finish their meal, and when they get up to leave, I watch the teen jut his chin forward and curl his lip as he lumbers out of the restaurant. In the two years that have passed since I last saw him, he has matured into a fine young douche. His mother has fully accepted that this is her son, and she seems okay with it. Well, she seems more okay with it after two glasses of wine. I look forward to the future when I will have been at the restaurant for twenty years, and he comes in with his own son, president of the Little Tykes Douche Bag Society. Only then will he fully understand what it's like to have a douche bag for a son.

CHAPTER FOUR

CUSTOMERS SAY THE DARNEDEST THINGS

SERVERS HEAR AND SEE A LOT. IT'S HARD TO believe what people will say or do while dining in a restaurant, not realizing that their companions aren't the only ones observing what's happening. Maybe after a few cocktails, the tongue gets a little looser and people are more comfortable sharing their true feelings, or maybe people don't care what their servers are finding out about them. I have learned a lot about some customers over the years, either by what I have heard or by their actions—and once I learn it, it's hard to forget.

Cloudy, with a Chance of "What the Fuck!"

We as servers are used to odd requests from guests who expect us to appease them in the name of good service. People seem to have no problem asking us to do things that may have nothing to do with the actual job we are hired to perform.

THERE ARE A PLENTY OF THINGS I DON'T MIND PEOPLE ASKING ME TO DO:

- Can I get a Jack and Coke on the rocks, but with the rocks on the side?

- Can you put the pickle on a separate plate because pickles freak me out when they touch my other food?

- Would you mind fixing the blinds so the sun doesn't shine in my eyes? I have an astigmatism and just had my eyes dilated.

- Can you put my mimosa in a coffee cup so nobody knows I am drinking?

- Can you wrap my food to go because I think this Reuben sandwich will taste better if I eat it at home after I get high?

THERE ARE A FEW THINGS THAT I CAN'T BELIEVE PEOPLE WILL ASK ME TO DO:

- Can you turn off the television over the bar because we don't allow our kids to watch TV when they eat?

- Would it be possible for you to run to the store and get some pancake syrup since I don't like maple?

- Would you mind watching my baby while I go to the bathroom?

- Will you taste this and tell me if you think it's good?

- Can you make me a double nonfat macchiato with low-fat chocolate syrup and the whipped cream on the side, with just a sprinkling of organic cinnamon, and then put it in a wineglass with a birthday candle on it?

The hostess Liz just shared with me a phone conversation that actually happened.

"Hello, I'm calling to get information about a performance happening there on December 4th, 5th, and 6th."

Liz, the ever-consummate professional, is eager to please and asks the caller what she needs to know. Performance times, ticket cost, directions to the club?

"Yes," the woman asks. "What is the *weather* going to be like on December 4th, 5th, and 6th?"

Lady, c'mon. This ain't the freaking Weather Channel. Did it sound like Sam Champion or Al Roker answered the phone? Did you dial 1-800-Accu-Weather Forecast? Seriously? But our hostess has a different list than I do regarding things she will and won't do in the name of good service. She actually goes onto the Internet and finds a weather forecast and relays the information to the lady. Liz is like our own personal meteorologist. The lady hangs up satisfied, and our hostess has proven, once again, that she is far better at that job than I am when asked to do it on occasion. Had I been the one to pick up the phone, the lady would have received a very different weather forecast.

"There is a 50 percent chance of I dunno with a humidity level of 100 percent and a cool front of apathy likely to come into our area at any moment. There is high-pressure system barreling down from the kitchen

Can someone please remind me which part of my job isn't real?

and ending up in my section, which is expected to bring with it showers of tears and patches of indifference, disregard, and aloofness. Highs will be in the low expectations, and the lows will be exceedingly disappointing."

WHAT I KNOW ABOUT THIS CUSTOMER: *She does not have a weather app on her cell phone.*

Sí, Señora: Soy Mexicano

Although I'm not certain, I think I was verbally assaulted at work by a racist. One of my regulars, who we all know is pretty much crazy, is a performer and quite well known. But this time she is here as a patron of the arts instead of standing on the stage and screeching out notes that were in her range about a decade ago. She wants me to know that she has just enjoyed dinner at a Mexican restaurant and has already sucked down two margaritas. In my attempt to make small talk, I tell her that I, too, enjoy Mexican food. She seems surprised, as if Mexican food is her little secret in the culinary world, and she can't believe that anyone else has ever heard of the exotic treat called a "taco."

"Sure, I love Mexican food," I tell her. "After all, I'm from Texas and I am half Mexican."

This comment, too, seems to take her by surprise. I'm not sure which part of the statement is so interesting, although I certainly don't appear to be your average Texan. I do not have a drawl, nor do I have a gun rack on the back window of my pickup truck.

"You're half Mexican?" She says this after sucking in her breath at an alarming rate. "I had no idea."

To be fair, you wouldn't necessarily think I was half Mexican, either, because I have fair skin and light eyes, but my last name, Cardosa, offers a clue. That, and my clinical addiction to tortillas and tequila.

Crazy Lady continues. "I can't believe you're half Mexican. You don't seem Mexican at all. You seem all *regular.*"

Wait, did this bitch just use the word *regular* to describe my race? *Regular* in the same way that "nude" pantyhose are considered "flesh-colored" by white people, and the way that crayons used to have a color called "flesh" that matched the skin of white people? Awww, hell no. I am about to reach into my pocket, pull out a handful of pinto beans, and rub them all up in her gringo face. Do not make me add another tear tattoo under my eye, because I may have to cut this bitch. (I will do the tattoo myself with a ballpoint pen, a needle, and lighter.) As I walk away, I hear

That moment your customer insults you, but you still need the tip, so you let it go.

her say to the table next to her, "Can you believe he is half Mexican?" So now my race is a topic of conversation among my whole section.

Growing up, I never knew which circle to fill in on the race classification section of various tests, which made the whole construct seem very odd to me. I never wanted to identify as White and disregard my dad or classify myself as Hispanic/Latino and ignore my mom, so I always checked the box marked "Other" and moved on. The next time I see Crazy Lady, though, I will put on my best Cheech-and-Chong accent and drive to her table in a low-rider while wearing a big fucking sombrero.

WHAT I KNOW ABOUT THIS CUSTOMER: *She may like Mexican food but she might not like Mexican people.*

Don't Squirt in My Eye

The woman who is walking into the club tonight has it all: a rich, good-looking husband; beautiful hair; a white leather skirt over her perfectly toned body; and a face pulled so tight I want to bounce a quarter off it just to see if I can catch it when it comes back at me. I can't tell if the sway in her walk is due to the alarmingly high stilettos she has squeezed her feet into or if it's from having too much to drink. I have a feeling it's a combination of both. She's a hot mess in a tight dress, but she's put together and I love it—an enigma wrapped in paraffin wax and coated with Botox® sprinkles.

The couple sits in my booth, and by the way she falls into it, I can tell that it is liquor that's making her wobble, and not so much the shoes. She rests her head on her wrist and cocks her cranium to the right so that her perfectly highlighted hair falls gracefully over her left eye, which is made up in one of those smoky raccoon-eye effects. I can't help but notice how her hair has wrapped itself around the dangling diamond earrings.

"Hello," she says. "And how are you tonight?"

"Very well, thank you. And how are you?"

She smiles at her husband in a way that makes me think she is about to give him an under-the-table hand job as I stand there with my order pad. "Oh, we're great. How are you?" she asks again.

"Very well, thank you. May I get you anything to drink? We do have a two-beverage minimum for the show tonight, but it doesn't have to be alcohol. I have bottled waters, sodas, juices, coffee, and tea as well." I want to make sure that this delicate flower knows she does not have to continue drinking alcohol if she chooses not to.

Her head teeters back and forth. Now that she is sitting and her body is no longer wobbling, her head is doing all the work.

"You know what I want? I want a vodka on the rocks with three limes. But can you squeeze the limes in for me? I just hate when anything shoots in my eye."

I look at her husband, who has a '70s porn vibe going on, and I can tell that he quite likes it when something shoots in her eye. Or at least on her face. He orders the same, and I go off to get their drinks.

Halfway through the show, they are ready for another round. I can tell because the husband has raised his right hand and is spinning his finger around in a circle repeatedly, in much the same way his wife's brain is probably doing inside her skull. I bring their second round, making sure to do what I can to avoid shooting anything in her eyes, although her eyelids are pulled so far back that, with the permanent squint, I find it hard to believe that anything gets into those eyes, ever. Not lime juice, sunlight, or reality.

A few minutes later, the man leaves his table and finds me at the bar. "Hey, can I get an ice pack?" he asks.

I try to remember where we keep the ice packs. I think they are in the dry goods storage right next to the IV drips, bandages, crutches, and bev naps.

"I'm sorry, I don't think I have one. Is everything all right?"

"Well, maybe you can just put some ice in a bag? My wife hurt her knee. I'm gonna go out and smoke a cigarette."

I find a plastic grocery bag to fill with ice and then place it inside another bag and take it to the woman, who is no longer at the table. It appears she has stumbled off to the restroom. I place the bag on the table and go back to the bar, where the woman approaches me a few minutes later, limping and brushing her hair out of her face with her meticulously manicured nails.

"I need an ice pack, honey? Do you have one?"

"Oh, your husband just asked me. I made one for you and it's at your table."

"Thanks, doll. I hurt my knee in a skeet accident yesterday, and then I just banged it against the table."

Wait, did she just tell me that she hurt her knee in a skeet accident? At first, I imagine she is referring to skeet shooting, the sport invented in 1920 where participants, using shotguns, attempt to break clay disks automatically flung into the air from two fixed stations at a high speed from a variety of angles. But then I think back to how she said she hates when things shoot into her eye, and I remember another definition for "skeet"—the one popularized by Lil John's hit "Get Low."

Now I am confused. Did she hurt her knee when she was shooting skeet or when she was skeeted upon? Either one is possible, I suppose. I choose to believe it's the latter and that the day before, sometime between her lunch social and her weekly hair appointment, her husband tried to skeet all up on her face, and she screamed out, "No! I'm getting a real facial tomorrow at the spa!" and fell off the leopard-print ottoman in her changing room, hurting her knee in the process. Yeah, that's totally it.

They eventually both return to the table, and she puts the ice pack on her knee. When it comes time to pay the bill, the husband whips out cash and hands it to me, giving $120 for his $90 check.

"Thank you very much, sir."

The wife then calls me over and hands me an additional $20 bill. "Thank you for everything. You're great." She attempts a wink, but it doesn't quite happen.

"Thank you very much, ma'am. Y'all have a great night."

WHAT I KNOW ABOUT THIS CUSTOMER: *She'll skeet, but she won't squirt.*

Lady at Table 56 Wants a (Sugar-Free) Rim Job

I am all for taking in fewer calories. It's not easy to maintain a slim figure when one is surrounded by fried foods and carbs at the job all day. For this reason, I always choose to have baked potato chips instead of the good ones, and I only eat half a doughnut and then blend the other half into a protein shake. It's little things like that that keep me trim and fit. I suppose every bit counts, but sometimes customers will try anything if they think it will save them from having to spend any time on the elliptical machine.

A woman wants a Lemon Drop martini. I, too, am a sucker for a Lemon Drop martini. Truth be told, I am a sucker for anything with the word "martini" in it. If someone created the Spinach and Kale martini, I might finally figure out a way to enjoy vegetables. A Lemon Drop is made with citrus vodka, triple sec, lemon juice, and served with a sugar rim. It can be all kinds of deliciousness if it's done right.

"Can you make a Lemon Drop martini for me?" the lady asks.

"Yes, ma'am. Would you like a sugar rim?"

Even though it always comes with a sugar rim, I get a kick out of asking people if they'd like it. It makes me think of Sheena Easton's song "Sugar Walls." When I was a kid, I never understood what a sugar wall was, but now I am pretty sure she was referring to the sweetness of her lady cavity.

The woman pauses a moment as she ponders the idea of a sugar rim. And then she says, "I'm trying to watch the calories. Can you do a sugar-free rim instead?"

"Of course, ma'am. The bartender would be pleased to rim your drink with a sugar substitute."

Is she serious? If she's trying to cut down on the calories, maybe she shouldn't be ordering a Lemon Drop martini in the first place. I look

JUST BECAUSE I'M NICE TO YOU DOESN'T MEAN I'M NOT MAKING FUN OF YOU IN THE KITCHEN.

up the calorie count for a Lemon Drop, and it ain't the sugar rim that's the problem.

Two ounces of Grey Goose Le Citron* vodka: 206 calories.

One ounce of triple sec: 125 calories.

Fresh lemon juice: calorie free.

One teaspoon of sugar (if you actually used that much for the rim job): 16 calories.

Total calories for this cocktail: 347.

If she switches to one teaspoon of a sugar substitute (4 calories) for her grainy, sweet sugar rim job, she will be saving all of 12 calories, which she already used up when she sucked down that bowl of hummus and then polished off the cracker crumbs by licking her finger and pressing it against the plate to get every last bit of food.

"Oh, he can give me a sugar-free rim?"

"Oh, he can give you a sugar-free rim, all right. The sweeter the rim, the better. If he can rim it, he will."

"That'll be great! I'd love a sugar-free rim!"

She looks relieved, as if she has just figured out a way to avoid hitting the gym tomorrow. The bartender gives her the rim job she wants, and it is so delicious and so "healthy" that she orders a second one, bringing her calorie total to 670. No word on how many calories are in the red velvet cake she splits with her friend . . .

People, don't pretend that you are on a diet and then drink cocktails. It makes no sense. And if you ask for something as ridiculous as a sugar-free rim on your cocktail, chances are good that your waiter is going to make fun of you behind your back fat, and maybe even write a story about it.

WHAT I KNOW ABOUT THIS CUSTOMER: *Her calorie-watching experiment isn't going very well.*

The Stupidest Reason Ever for Not Leaving a Tip

We servers are asked to do a lot for our customers in order to earn the tips that we receive. Many people seem to keep a mental checklist of things we should do, and as soon as we miss one of them, they have the justification they need to make themselves feel better about leaving a big fat zero of a tip. I can understand how some folks one would want to leave less than 20 percent if their server never filled an empty glass of water, but we know there are people who have had their glass filled ten times, but because there was no eleventh time, the tip is reduced. Or how about that customer who leaves a bad tip because he said the waitress didn't smile enough? Never mind that the waitress got the food out in a timely manner, was efficient and prompt, and never made any gaffes. "She didn't seem happy enough while serving me, so no tip for her!" I know one waitress who got stiffed, and the customer let her know why at the bottom of the signed receipt he left her: "Learn to flirt a little bit, and maybe you'll get better tips."

Why the fuck does a waitress have to learn to flirt to deserve a tip? Isn't it enough that she made sure your goddamn burger came out just the way you wanted it—medium rare but without too much pink and instead of fries you want a salad but only if the salad is with baby greens, and if you can't have baby greens then you want sautéed spinach with no oil or butter, and you want bacon but first you need to know where it was sourced from because you can only eat bacon that came from a farm with happy pigs who were slaughtered while listening to classical music. So after the waitress gets your fucking food right, you want her to tilt her head back and laugh while she bats her fucking eyelashes at you, is that it? You're only gonna leave a tip if she puts on some extra lip gloss and lets her breasts rub against your shoulder as she refills your iced tea? Or do you want her to talk in a little girl voice as she describes the dessert specials and then tell you how much she loves to eat chocolate in bed or while taking a bubble bath? Fuck you.

I'm not flirting with you.

I'm earning my tip.

Why don't you just tip the waitress for the job she did and keep your blue balls out of the decision-making process when it comes time to tip? The check the waitress was stiffed on was for $12.05, so if you can't afford the $2.10 the tip should have been, you should just cop to the fact that you're a cheap asshole who had no intention of leaving a tip in the first place. Save your stupid fucking advice about learning how to flirt and take your ass to a strip club where the women will flirt with you all you want, as long as you put dollar bills in their G-strings.

Please tip your servers based on the job they do for you. If they didn't bring you your food or if they forgot everything you asked for, that's one thing. But if, in the course of the meal, your waitress never winks at you or pantomimes giving a blow job, that doesn't mean she's a bad waitress. Put your hand in your pocket, push your tiny penis out of the way, and grab a couple of dollars to thank your professional, nonhooker waitress for putting up with a pompous sleazeball lowlife like yourself.

WHAT I KNOW ABOUT THIS CUSTOMER: *He doesn't have a girlfriend, and it's no wonder.*

Shut the Fuck Up

There is a guy who often comes into the restaurant and always stays up to forty-five minutes after we close. He couldn't catch a clue if it were covered in Super Glue®. Candles extinguished, floors being mopped, cooks scrubbing walls, and this guy nurses his cocktail for eternity. When he graced us with his presence recently, I got to listen to him talk for the whole length of my shift. Yes, I am truly saying that he was blabbing his mouth when I punched in and his engine was still running when I punched out and said good-bye four hours later. It really boggles my mind that he can talk incessantly about absolutely nothing and not even realize that he's making the people around him feel trapped, miserable, suicidal, and brain dead. As he yammers on, you feel a pang of sympathy for each victim who innocently sits next to him at the bar and ends up being caught in his trap of conversation. They try to send signals for rescue. Their eyes are saying things like "Why is this guy talking to me?" and "Isn't my table ready yet?" and "Can someone please inject my veins with liquid drain cleaner and help me die a little bit faster?" It's really sad. I took a few notes on the things that he bores us with, so you know what I am forced to listen to:

- He gives a play-by-play description of a video that he saw on the Internet about a dog. He reenacts the whole thing to an unfortunate lady who was casually waiting for her friend. I saw the video. Everyone saw it. It is a two-minute video on the Internet but his interpretation of it is at least three times as long.

- He gives a rundown of all the zoos in New York City, including the Bronx Zoo, the Central Park Zoo, and the one in Brooklyn. He tells us which days are the best to go visit and how much they cost. He also has some thoughts about certain animals being held in captivity. He aggressively believes that polar bears should never, ever, under any circumstances, be held in captivity. No word on how he feels about black bears, brown bears, grizzly bears, koala bears, panda bears, or the Sri Lankan sloth bear, but polar bears should *definitely* never ever be held in captivity.

- He gives us a dissertation on the various brick-oven pizzas in and around New York City, because, you know, he's an expert on brick-oven pizzas.

- He tells us the proper way to cook garlic, and here's a news flash: You don't want it to get too brown. Thanks for the tip, Monsieur Chef.

- He goes into a diatribe about the royal wedding of Prince William and Kate Middleton. He thinks Kate is prettier than Princess Diana was, and when discussing Kate's sister, Pippa, he has some very strong opinions. I quote: "How dare that bitch wear a white dress at her sister's wedding!"

When it is time for me to leave, I give a simple prayer of thanks that I have escaped without ever having his words directed at me. If you look at Medusa, you turn to stone. If you look at this guy, you spend the rest of the night wishing that your feet were tied to a bag of stones being thrown into the East River. Death, take me away.

WHAT I KNOW ABOUT THIS CUSTOMER: *Too damn much.*

Your Nuts Are My Pleasure

You know I work in a totally classy establishment, right? I know it's classy because we have candles on every table, our martinis cost $15, and we wear all-black uniforms. Class-A, indeed. A gentleman calls me over to his table during the performance and I assume he needs another glass of our top-notch Pinot Noir, or maybe he wants an order of our Poisson d'Or des Biscottes that are a steal at $6.50 for an itty-bitty portion that we pour into a tiny glass bowl directly from the giant tub of Goldfish® crackers we bought wholesale. I lean in to find out what he'd like, and he whispers into my ear something decidedly un-classy.

"Can you turn down the air-conditioning? I'm freezing my nuts off. I ain't lying."

I am shocked. Shocked, I tell you! Why does this older gentleman with his distinguished gray hair and fancy suit feel it necessary to assault my virgin ears with such a horrific expression? Never mind the fact that it is about ninety degrees outside and we need that air-conditioning going full blast. Never mind that he is in the company of a lady friend who would surely be appalled by such disturbing vocabulary. What I find most shocking is that this old man even knows that his testicles are still there. They probably hang so low that one of them is tucked into his sock. They are probably covered in so much gray that a whole vat of men's hair-dye formula would surrender at the challenge. Nevertheless, he is worried that his nuts will get so cold that they will shrivel up, fall off, and roll away under Booth 6—never to be seen again until I sweep there. (So, never.) Since I have all the care and concern in the world for this man's family jewels, I rush to the thermostat and raise the temperature. I do not want to be held responsible for a man losing his precious nuts. Be they acorn, betel, pecan, walnut, cashew, almond, filbert, or beech, I do not need that responsibility.

About ten minutes later I go to check on the temperature of his testicles.

"Sir, is everything better now? How are they hangin'?"

He assures me that all is fine down below. I shake off the mental image and remove his empty wineglass and ask if he'd like another. He does. I bring it. We are good.

As he leaves, he thanks me again for adjusting the A/C. On the table is a good tip, but I have received more from him than just 20 percent. I have learned something. Thanks to Mr. Icy Nuts, I know now that even though I work at a place that is as classy as all get out, sometimes the riffraff will sneak in. Underneath their fine Italian suits and rigid demeanor, we sometimes have a guy who has no problem talking to me about his balls.

WHAT I KNOW ABOUT THIS CUSTOMER: *He likes warm balls and he cannot lie.*

Caught in a Cougar Trap

It's been so long since anything like this has happened to me, so maybe I am mistaken, but I think I just got hit on. I am at work, minding my own business, leaning against the bar trying to find the breeze of the air conditioner that the owner of the restaurant swears is turned on. The lady at the end of the bar glances my way. I smile at her because I am in customer service and I smile at anybody who makes eye contact with me. My face is saying, "I am happy to be here. How can I help you?" while my brain is saying, "Take this steak knife out of my hand before I end it all right here by slicing my wrists and then have to mop the blood off the floor before I expire." I move behind the bar to retrieve the order that is coming out of the printer. It's for a glass of wine, so I decide to be a team player and pour it, since the bartender is busy updating his status on social media.

"You pour that wine very nicely," says the lady, her eyes lingering on me a little longer than what feels comfortable.

"Years of practice," I say. "Although at my apartment it usually comes out of a box and gets poured into a jelly jar."

"Is that your natural hair?" she asks me.

"Yep, this is it," I say, as if anyone would go to the wig store and look for the biggest, frizziest, bird's nest–looking mess of hair and exclaim, "That's the hair for me!"

"Well, it's adorable. How do you make it do that?"

"I wash it and go like this." I shake my head back and forth making my hair even bigger than it was to begin with, ignoring the three or four stray hairs that fall onto the cutting board for the bread.

"Well, you're so cute, you could do whatever you want."

She takes another sip of her dirty martini, and while she is trying to fish the olive from the bottom of her glass with her tongue, I take my chance to run away. I know her type. She's alone at a bar and is willing to have a conversation with anyone who will listen to her. I am not willing. I give a cursory check to Table 7 and decide I need to hang out someplace where bored customers won't try to talk to me. After playing my turns

on a word game and making a phone call in the bathroom, I am forced back to the bar—the only place in the restaurant that gives the illusion of air-conditioning. There she is, on martini number two and scanning the room for someone to listen to her. Her eyes fall on me.

"Did you come back here so you could be close to me?" she asks.

"No, the A/C." I flip my hair out of my eyes and hope that our conversation is over.

"Well, just so you know, I wouldn't kick you out of bed."

This is my cue to get the fuck away from the crazy delusional lady who needs glasses—and I'm not talking about the martini kind. "Good to know," I say. "I'll keep that in mind."

I head directly to the kitchen where I can shake off the thought of the middle-aged woman lounging in my bed with a postcoital cigarette and a dirty martini as she scans my room for manly artifacts, like the framed picture of Judy Garland hanging on my Tiffany'-blue walls. Maybe I am reading too much into our conversation, but there is a definite "Mrs. Robinson" vibe going on. I am scared to go back to the bar, but the lure of pseudo–air-conditioning gets the better of me and I am again standing close to my would-be suitor. Her second martini is almost a memory now, and I watch her swallow the last little bit. She licks her lips and pulls out a lipstick from her ratty purse that looks like it was a free prize at the 1964 World's Fair. She slathers the lipstick on—a shade probably called Rouge de Cougar, or Desperation Rosewood—and watches me all the while. She puts on enough lipstick for at least three pairs of lips.

I stare back at her just because I want to play the game. I also want to stay in the piddling stream of air-conditioning. I wonder what she expects to get by coming on to a waiter. Perhaps she thinks I will rip my apron off and carry her downstairs to the storage room, where we will make sweet love on some broken-down cardboard boxes next to the giant cans of ketchup. Or maybe she hopes that my shift is almost over and I will follow her back to her pad, no doubt decorated with zebra-print scarves thrown over lampshades and a stereo console playing Tom Jones records.

"Well, I guess I'll be on my way," she tells me as she picks up her glass of water for one final wetting of the whistle. When she puts the glass back down, it has a lipstick smear on it that will require a paper towel and some major elbow grease to remove.

"Have a good night, ma'am," I chirp. I wave good-bye and smile at her in a way that will let her think that if I was off work, fifteen years older, and straight, she just might have a chance with me. "See you next time."

She gets off her barstool and exits the restaurant alone. The door closes behind her faster than she expects it to and catches the heel of her shoe, causing her to let out a final flirtatious yelping sound. She waves at me through the window and is then out of sight.

So, was she hitting on me? Yeah, I think she was. Did she strike out? Yes, she did. Do I still got it? Abso-fucking-lutely.

WHAT I KNOW ABOUT THIS CUSTOMER: *Her gaydar is broken.*

The Softer Side of Bitch

HOW TO THAW OUT A BITCHY HEART

It is my regular Thursday night shift, and we have a new bartender. The last one, BJ, only lasted two weeks before the manager let him go for complaining too much, not being friendly to the people who sat at his bar, and once making a mojito with salt instead of sugar. I questioned whether he should have been fired for a simple mistake like mixing up the identical plastic containers of salt and sugar, but the manager told me that after he sent the drink out, he knew he had made the mistake and just decided to "wait and see if they would notice it or not." Of course they noticed. Fired.

The new bartender is named Matt, and he's a nice-enough guy. I'm not in a great mood to begin with and seeing yet another bartender here means that I will spend the evening having to answer the same questions I have been answering for two weeks with BJ. Having a new bartender makes my mood dip a little bit lower than it was when I left home for work. We make the obligatory small talk for the first thirty minutes of the shift until our first customers come in. This being a neighborhood restaurant, Matt happens to know them. It is an older man and his wife, and they are joined by a younger woman.

"Hello, Tom!" Matt says from behind the bar. "Have a seat, and I'll get you some menus."

Matt is already friendlier than BJ ever was, and he places three menus at Booth 8. As Matt walks back behind the bar, he whispers in my ear.

"That's my former neighbor and his wife. She has dementia, so you might have to be a bit patient with them."

I look over at the couple, and the man is very sweetly taking the coat off his wife, who has a beaming smile and is scanning the room for signs of something or someone familiar. It takes a few minutes for them to sit down, so I watch how gingerly this man treats his wife. You can see in his eyes the amount of love he has for her, and it's easy to tell that he does not mind one bit that he may have to do more for her now than he used to. The woman sitting across from them seems like a family friend.

When I approach the table, I realize that the smile on my face is different than it usually is when I'm at work: It's real. I want to make sure that this woman gets the best possible experience from me, and I want to do everything I can to ensure that she is happy for the next half an hour. The husband orders some coffee.

"I haven't made any yet, but I'll start it right now so it will be really fresh for you," I say. "What about you, ma'am, would you like some coffee?"

She smiles at me but doesn't answer my question. She looks like she is wondering if I am someone she met before and should recognize, and I so badly want to tell her, "It's okay. You don't know me. It's fine."

The friend asks her if she wants coffee, and she eventually nods her head, yes. The husband orders a cheeseburger, as does the friend, and then they ask the woman if she would like one, too. Again, she nods her head, yes.

"Would you like cheddar cheese or American cheese?" I ask her.

"Yes," she says.

The husband answers for her, so I ring in three burgers with cheddar, all medium well. When I return with the coffee, the man thanks me for the piping-hot freshness of it, and when he pours the cream into his cup, I notice that his hands are trembling in that way so many elderly hands do. He dutifully pours the cream into his wife's cup, stirs it, and then slides the cup in front of her.

All I want to do for this table is smile. I want to make eye contact with this woman and let her know that someone is out here who wants her to be happy. Whether she understands me or not, I want to talk to her.

Their food comes out, and the woman eats every last bite of her burger. Her husband and her friend congratulate her for doing such a good job with her plate, and she again responds, "Yes." But she is smiling. Always smiling.

As they get up to go, I watch the husband help his wife with her coat and scarf. I see her look at him as if she surely must know who he is. If not, she at least knows that it's someone who loves her very much.

"Thank you," I say to all three of them. "And have a great night," I tell the woman.

She returns my comment with another smile that makes me feel grateful. I want her to remember the time she went to a restaurant and the waiter was so nice to her. If nothing else, she knew for that very moment that someone was being kind to her, and, like a flash, that moment was gone for her.

Once they leave, I realize that her smile will be one of those memories I hope never slips away. I also never want to forget her husband's demonstration of real, transcendent love. And maybe I can recall that memory the next time I feel a bit discouraged about having to work with another new bartender.

·～◦◦◦～·

CHAPTER FIVE

WHEN I EAT CROW, I LIKE IT WELL DONE

AS STATED IN THE FIRST CHAPTER, THE CUSTOMER is not necessarily always right. Well, neither am I. As hard as it is for me to admit this, there have been times when I have been wrong. Don't misunderstand me: I'm not going to own up to every single mistake I make. If I can figure out a way to conceal an error and make it appear as if I am the perfect server, then that is what I am going to do. However, on occasion, I might do the wrong thing.

Don't Make Me Throw a Penny at You

I am working at a tourist trap in Times Square where the food is way overpriced but tourists come anyway because it is familiar. It is the lunch rush, and in my station are three women who appear to have come from their office jobs. Judging by the way they bark at me, it seems they are happy to have someone to boss around for a change. I assume they are secretaries who are perpetually put upon. They order their usual salads with everything on the side but extra everything and lemons for the waters and separate checks and anything else that screams, "We are needy, high-maintenance bitches." It is a busy Wednesday when everyone in the restaurant has tickets to see *Cats* or *Phantom of the Opera* or anything else that screams, "We are eager, high-maintenance tourists." After a while, the three secretaries call me over to their table.

"Is our food ready yet? It's been about twenty-five minutes and we're on our lunch break," says one lady with feathered hair and lip liner.

I hate when people ask if their food is ready, because if it were ready it would be on their table. We are not in the habit of keeping completed orders in the kitchen until the customer reminds us that they still want it.

"The kitchen is a little backed up today, but I'll go check on your food."

I step over to the computer to look at what time the order was rung in and see it has only been sixteen minutes and not twenty-five. That is not a long enough time for me to question the kitchen about food, so I go to another table to fill water glasses instead. As I am pouring, I see Ms. Feathered Hair waving at me, so I head back to see what she needs now.

"Ummm, you said you were going to go check on our food and you didn't. We have been waiting for almost half an hour. Is our food ready or not?"

By this point, they have already whined that they didn't have enough lemons and that we didn't have what they wanted and that the prices are too high.

My fuse is short, so I reply, "If your food was ready, it would be here, okay? So I guess it's not. And it hasn't been thirty minutes, it's been sixteen." I walk away to go hover in the kitchen until their lunch is ready.

Their food comes out, and they complain about the usual things needy high-maintenance bitches complain about: My bread isn't warm enough, my diet soda tastes flat, no one wants to sleep with me because I'm stuck-up . . .

I put their check down and go on with my other tables. When they get up to leave, I notice they have left money on the table to pay for the check, and I know what to expect: exact change, no tip. But then I see my tip: one penny in the bottom of a glass of water. I fish it out and scan the room for them. They are already gone, so I run downstairs out to the street and

That moment a customer threatens to never come back and you're totally okay with it.

look both ways. I have to decide whether to go left or right. I decide on the right and run east down the street, penny in hand. About halfway to Sixth Avenue I see them. After knocking a couple of tourists out of the way, I go to the head secretary bitch and tap her on the shoulder.

"You forgot something at your table," I say.

"Oh, I did? What?"

"This," and I flick the penny at her.

Suddenly everything is in slow motion. I watch the copper coin twirl through the air as her face recoils in terror. The penny hits her tit and bounces to the sidewalk. I turn around to walk back to the restaurant giddy with pride, but she is right behind me. I can hear her high heels click-clacking on the sidewalk, and I can practically feel her hot honey-mustard breath on the back of my neck.

When I get back inside, I head straight to the bathroom to hide out, because I know I am about to be in big trouble. After a few minutes of crouching in a stall, a coworker finds me and says that the manager needs to see me right away. I slink into her office, ready to be berated. My manager shuts the door and turns around, and I am surprised to see that she has a huge smile on her face. She tells me that even though the bitches deserved to have a penny thrown at them, what I did was wrong. She is going to have to suspend me for three days, so that all of my coworkers know that throwing pennies at customers is not acceptable behavior for our fine-dining establishment. Now I wish I had thrown a whole roll of pennies at the woman so it *really* would have been worth my while.

My response to being suspended for three days? "Okay, got it. Can I cash out now because it looks like I have a three-day-weekend ahead of me?"

After my three days off, I return to work as a hero. A legend. A penny-throwing hero legend.

One Fancy-Ass Dessert, Comin' Right Up

Over time, it has become clear to me that the world is a better place when people own up to their mistakes. For instance, if I forget to ring in an order and Table 12's well-done burger sits on the pad in my apron for ten minutes before I remember to ring it in, I am flat-out honest with the table and tell them why their food is taking so long. It's better than blaming it on the kitchen or some other bullshit excuse. I think it makes a table appreciate my honesty—and then tip me better.

When I get to work, I look at the list of specials and try to commit them to memory. Nobody wants to hear their server read a list of specials off a piece of paper. It takes about two minutes to memorize the four specials, so I do it in order to appear more professional to my guests. The chef sometimes just tells us what the dessert specials are going to be and writes them down later in the evening. One of the desserts is something I have never heard of—something called a "clafoutis." The chef describes it as a classic warm cranberry dessert that is similar to a custardlike cake. He mumbles the name of the dessert one time, but he fails to tell me that it is French—I don't learn that vital piece of information until after my shift. After my first table of the evening is finished with their meal, I approach them with a dessert menu and began to explain what the specials are. As I begin my description of the mysterious dessert, I suddenly cannot remember what it is called. I haven't written it down, so I just go for it: I call it a "flatooey." Yes, a flatooey. I may as well have called it a shipoopi. Or a Zamboni®. I say it with confidence, like there really is a fancy fucking dessert called a flatooey. The man at the table starts laughing when I say it, and my stupid ass thinks he is laughing with me, not at me. I give him a look that says, "I know, isn't that the craziest name for a dessert you have ever heard?" I laugh, having no idea he probably knows that I am trying to say "clafoutis" and not "flatooey."

I go on to several more tables with my lack of French dessert knowledge and return to the board to see what kind of sauce the other dessert comes with. That is when I realize I have been totally mispronouncing the

Dessert is a dish best served with correct pronunciation.

fancy dessert all night long. It strikes me as funny, and I start to giggle. The chef asks me why I am laughing, but I don't dare tell him that I have been totally botching up his dessert description. Years and years in the restaurant business, and here I am felled by the pronunciation of one single dessert.

My humble upbringing has bitten me hard in the ass on this night. My childhood diet of Ding Dongs®, Pop-Tarts®, and candy bars has not prepared me for a centuries-old fancy-ass dessert called a clafoutis. I attempt to correct my pronunciation, but I still am not certain I am saying it the right way. For the rest of the night, I pronounce it as if I'm in Texas: "Why hi thar, folks, Maybe y'all'd like to try this high falutin' dessert we gots tonight called a 'clawfootie.' It shore is good. Granny done cooked it up in the backyard next to the cement pond. Y'all come back now, ya hear?"

God, I'm an idiot. When I get home that night, I look up the term and learn the proper way to say it. By the way, I also learn that, since it was served with cranberries and not cherries, the dessert is technically called a "flaugnarde." So I wasn't the only one who was wrong that night, Chef Know-It-All.

How to Scam Free Food

There is an age-old custom at many chain restaurants of giving your tables a survey or comment card to fill out to see if they had wonderful service and enjoyed their crappy precooked food. Although I am not a fan of these surveys, there is a way you can make them work for you, rather than against you. It just takes some effort and some stamps.

When I was working in lovely Times Square, we were always busy with tons of tourists who came into the restaurant because of its familiarity. Don't ask me why anyone would get into an airplane and travel hundreds or thousands of miles only to end up eating dinner at a place that is also in their local mall, but people did. I guess once they're in New York, they get so homesick that they need nachos and spinach dip calorie bombs. It wasn't very often that people would take the time to fill out the comment cards, but plenty of people would ask to speak to a manager to complain about the quality of the food or their service. It was always surprising to me when people thought their steak or salmon tasted less than ideal or that they thought the service was subpar. C'mon, it's a franchise restaurant in Times Square, for fuck's sake. Of course it sucked. Eventually, I had enough of people dissing my service. Granted, my service may have sucked, but I was sick of people telling my manager about it. I devised a plan—a very special bitchy-waiter plan.

One night I decide to type a letter from a family of "customers," praising my serving skills. I go on and on about how I went above and beyond their expectations, how I recommended what they would like the most on the menu, and then how delicious the food was. I even write a fictional paragraph about how good I was with their children—how I made them laugh and finish their veggies. I also write that I suggested which Broadway shows they would enjoy. Basically, I write that I was an angel sent from heaven to serve in Times Square. I then place that letter into a stamped envelope and address it to the restaurant. Then I place that envelope into another envelope and send it to my friend who lives in Georgia. When Ron gets the letter, all he has to do is drop it back into a mailbox so it will be postmarked from Georgia, and no one would ever suspect that I wrote it about myself.

A few days later, the letter appears. My manager is elated. She is so proud of me that she staples the letter to the bulletin board so all the other servers can see what high standards they need to live up to. I am the superstar waiter of Times Square. A couple of people know that I wrote the letter, but most people just can't believe that someone would write such a glowing review about me. But there it is in black and white, hanging in the kitchen and postmarked from Georgia—it *must* be true.

The letter stays there for a few weeks. Best of all, my manager rewards me with a $50 gift card for another franchise restaurant, and all it cost me was about ten minutes of time and two stamps. It really is one of my proudest moments. My manager would be so disappointed if she knew the truth: There is no family in Athens, Georgia who loves me. I'm sorry, Gladys, but thank you for the free food.

SOMETIMES I GO ONLINE
AND WRITE GOOD REVIEWS
ABOUT MYSELF.

Dear Bitchy,

I work in a restaurant and have been doing the classic rollup for years. The problem is that the flap hangs out and doesn't always keep the silverware tight in the rollup. There was a person I worked with who rolled the silverware so that everything got tucked into the rollup and it wouldn't come unwrapped, but I can't remember how he did it! Do you know how to do that? If not, where should I look?

Signed,
David

Dear David,

I do know of this secret technique you speak of. Are you referring to the one where all the corners of the napkin are somehow practically invisible, and the rollup remains tight, even as it is stacked and then carried to a drawer or bin? The technique was taught to me by a Buddhist monk who lived in a cave in the mountains of the Himalayas. He was on a forty-year vow of silence, and all he did was eat, pray, and do rollups. I went to this guru once so he could show me the art of mastering the rollup. Unfortunately, I made a solemn pledge to him that I would only pass on his technique to people who worked with me and could volunteer to do my sidework for three weeks in exchange for the coveted information. Sorry, David. Besides, the place I work now is a class-act, super-fancy place that uses paper napkins, so I very rarely practice the rollup technique anymore. Had you asked me how to wrap a to-go item in foil into the shape of swans, geese, elephants, puppies, goldfish, Mariah Carey, antelopes, or cantaloupes, I would happily explain to you the proper technique. But you didn't, so I won't.

I do apologize that I am unable to give you the information you so desperately crave. The monk's name was Maha-Thera Sayagyi U Ba "Scooter" Khin, and I know he would be very disappointed in me if I shared his knowledge. I am sure you understand, right, David? If you are unable to find someone to help you with this matter, I would suggest you take a quick trip over to Asia. There is a La Quinta® in the foothills of the Himalayas that has a pretty good rate and a free continental breakfast. The front desk can direct you to which cave Scooter lives in. Tell him I said hello. By the way, if you go, don't forget that Scooter is on a vow of silence, so don't expect a lot of chitchat. Good luck!

Mustard and mayo,

The Bitchy Waiter

What Would You Do?

Every day we are faced with decisions that can alter the course of our lives. Do I take the N train or do I walk the extra block to the F train? Do I use the money in my checking account to pay my electricity bill, or do I go buy the latest tablet computer? Tequila or vodka with dinner? (The answer to the last question, all too often, is "both.") In the restaurant industry, we are also given the task of deciding things, and sometimes it's not easy to know what the best choice will be. Should I take Table 7's order now, or should I run the drinks to Table 14 first? Do I hide my coffee cup of Chardonnay behind the bread warmer or on the shelf next to the to-go boxes? Do I ignore that crying baby or do I hand it a steak knife and a bottle of hot sauce and hope for the best? All of these are important decisions, but one event happens in the course of every server's life that becomes not just any decision but a moral one.

It is a very busy night at the restaurant. I am the only server and we have no busser or food runner, meaning I am doing it all, except for making the drinks. It must be a slow night on television, which, coupled with the abnormally warm weather for early March, makes for a slammed night. Every time I turn around, there is another party waiting at the door to be seated. Tables are dirty and I am a madman. I actually really like it when it's this way; I tend to do better in a pressure situation. My smile goes into hyperdrive, and I wait tables like a well-oiled machine. The food is coming out quickly, and the customers are all satisfied. Maybe they have to wait a little longer than usual, but I have found that if I at least reach out to those customers and let them know that I know they are there, it makes it okay. "Hi, folks. I'm a bit busy but gimme a minute and I'll be right back with a water pitcher, and I will take your order," I say over and over again. Repeatedly, I hear comments like "I can't believe you're the only one here, you're amazing!" and "You are doing such a great job!" and "Your hair is gorgeous." I relish these compliments—as long as they are backed up with 20 percent tips.

At one point, I have food in the window, tables to clear, he needs a beer, waters to fill, she needs her bill, orders to take, coffee to make,

We don't believe in the three-second rule. We use the three-minute rule.

people to seat . . . Madness! And then: "Excuse me. Can you wrap this steak up for me? Thanks."

"Absolutely, ma'am. I'll be right back."

I take the plate from her hand and run to the back sidestand, where we keep the to-go boxes (and tonight, my coffee cup of Chardonnay). While holding the plate, I bend over to pick up a box from the shelf and watch the half-eaten steak slide slowly from the plate onto the floor that, although mopped by myself just a couple of hours earlier, was certainly not clean enough to eat off. This is what we call a moral decision.

Do I take the steak from the floor, citing the "three-second rule," and put it in the to-go box and carry it back to the woman? Or do I go to the chef and explain that I need another well-done steak but I only need half of it, and I need it ten minutes ago? Who will know if I put the dirty steak in the box? As long as I brush off any dust bunnies and/or crumbs, nobody. The chef will be pissed off if I ask him to make another steak, especially in the middle of a rush like this. He'll make me pay for it, both financially and mentally, and that ain't gonna happen.

Will the lady get sick if she eats the dirty steak? Maybe it's for her dog, anyway. Maybe the chef will understand, but that seems highly unlikely. What to do, what to do? I pick up the dirty meat and place it gently into the to-go box and close the lid. Should I give it to her? Maybe I can just tell her what happened and then offer her a dessert on the house instead. Or maybe she'll say it doesn't matter because it's for her step-daughter's lunch tomorrow and she doesn't like her stepdaughter much anyway. Maybe when I go to tell her, she will get totally pissed off at me and make a big scene, and I could have avoided the whole thing by giving her the meat right off the floor.

I look over at the chef, who is yelling at another cook about how he had just wasted two pieces of bacon by overcooking them. I look at the lady, who is laughing at her friend's joke and finishing her third glass of Cabernet. I look at my coffee cup of Chardonnay and take a swig. I close the lid of the box and write on top of it, "Enjoy!" I'm still not sure if the box will ever make it to the woman. Maybe I'll just tell her it fell on the floor and will get her another glass of wine. But then I'll have to tell my boss that I need a glass of wine comped, and this is the man who won't even let me have French fries. I place the to-go box into a bag and finish off my Chardonnay. This is a moral dilemma. I know I shouldn't give her the steak, but I am fearful of the repercussions if I tell her the truth. I look for the angel and devil that are usually sitting on my shoulders to see which way my conscience should guide me, but the only thing I see on my shoulder is a smear of ketchup from when I was filling the bottles earlier and one of them exploded. Slowly, I pick up the bag of dirty meat and leave the sidestand, still unsure of what I will do. As I head toward her table, I see the trash can to my right and the customer to my left. Which one do I choose?

Never Judge a Man by his Mom Jeans

I first met this interesting couple at the restaurant about a year ago. The two sat down in my station, and they each ordered a glass of wine. As I am taking the order, I assume the two are lesbians. The slightly more feminine of the two asks for a Chardonnay, and the "butch" one orders a Merlot. I wonder if they are sisters, life partners, or just a couple of lady-loving ladies on their way to an Indigo Girls concert, with a brief stop at the home improvement store. I am a little busy, and the bartender tells me that I accidentally picked up a Pinot Grigio instead of the requested Chardonnay. I figure I will wait and see if they even notice. Two minutes later, I am called over to the table where one of them says, "I do believe this is something other than Chardonnay." She licks her chapped lips and sniffs the inside of her glass. "Perhaps it's a Pinot Grigio, but definitely not a Chardonnay. Can you double-check that I got the right glass of wine, please?"

Color me impressed.

Upon closer inspection, I see that the two have matching wedding bands, so I know now that they are not sisters

"Are you folks ready to order?" I ask.

Chardonnay Lady says, "Well, I know what I want, but he might need a little more time."

I do not hear what she says after that because I am trying to understand why, if this is her husband, and he is a man, he is wearing a pair of mom jeans. I look closer at the husband as he takes a swallow of his Merlot, and I see the bobbing of an Adam's apple in his throat.

Color me surprised.

The couple comes in on occasion over the next year. They are never rude but never friendly, not smiling but not frowning, either. I always make sure to pick up Chardonnay, and I have to remind myself not to say, "Hello, ladies." He really does look like a woman. Remember Miss Jane Hathaway from *The Beverly Hillbillies*? He looks like her, but maybe not quite so masculine.

Last week, the couple came in again. It is a hot, humid day, and they sit at Booth 9 and order their usual wines. A few minutes later, another

couple who had been sitting on the patio comes inside to finish their bottle of rosé in the air-conditioning. When they walk past the couple at Booth 9, Mom Jeans says to the man, "Hey, real men don't drink rosé."

"When it's this hot outside, they do," the man counters as he heads to the bar. They are obviously friends, but the exchange is surreal and confounding: a woman-shaped man is calling another man's manhood into question, after all. Do real men only drink Merlot? Do real men have bottoms shaped like pears? Do real men wear mom jeans? I am confused.

"Well, I guess we can make an exception then," says Pear Bottom. "It *is* hot, after all."

The rosé-drinking man laughs and sits his decidedly un-pearlike ass onto a barstool. Mom Jeans takes another swig of his Merlot and orders another. His wife asks for a second Chardonnay and gives me the look that says, "Don't fuck it up again," even though I only messed up that one time, and it was over a year ago. It's our thing now, I guess.

At the end of the night, I get a 20 percent tip, and I am secure in knowing that for every pair of mom jeans, there is a pear-shaped ass ready to fill them—and sometimes that pear-shaped ass might belong to a man who looks more like a woman than Miss Jane Hathaway.

Tattoo Fail

As servers, we are required on a daily basis to make conversation with complete strangers. Do we like doing that? Of course not. We would be more than happy to simply ask the important questions like "Do you want fries with that?" and "Do you need change?" but sometimes we feel obligated to say something like "How are you today?" or "Wow, look at the mess your baby made. That's cute." Small talk is part of the job, and making banal conversation is a way to increase tips because it shows the customer that we are making a meaningful connection with them. Yeah, uh-huh. I suspect that bartenders have to try even harder to act like they want to talk to customers since they are trapped behind the counter. We may not truly care about the personal lives of our customers, but we do our best to make it seem as if we dig deep into our aprons and find one more fuck to give. Personally, my apron has been pretty much out of fucks since 1998, and so is this bartender's who is serving me.

By the time I pour myself into her barstool, I am well on my way to a very decent hangover. I had started drinking mojitos a couple of hours before at a different bar, and then I decided it was a good idea to order a frozen drink that has three different kinds of rum in it and is the color of the Caribbean on acid.

The bartender is an edgy-looking chick covered with tattoos. Her smile is way too bright for my prehangover eyes. She makes my drink efficiently and sets it down before me. I notice that she has an abstract tattoo on her left wrist that is very similar in position to the one on my right forearm.

"Nice tattoo," I say, forgetting that she might dislike talking to customers as much as I do. "What does it mean?"

She immediately places her right hand over it, obscuring it from my view. "It's a private symbol." She gives a smug little smile, bats her eyelashes, flips her hair, and walks away from me, effectively shutting down that conversation. I am left sitting at the bar feeling like an asshole for trying to get all up in her private world. I take a sip of my frozen blue cocktail and scrape off some of the frost from the outside of the glass. And then I think, *"Listen, if you want to have a private symbol tattooed on your body that you don't want to share with anyone else, then maybe you shouldn't have it on your left wrist, where everyone in the world can see it. Why don't you tattoo that bullshit on your inner thigh, so you can select who will get to look at it."*

My tattoo is pretty personal, too, but I don't feel the need to shut down when people ask me what it means. Mine is of an arrow on my right forearm pointing to my hand. I got it one year after one of my closest friends died of cancer. His name was Van, and I knew him for over twenty years. I could always depend on him for anything, whether I needed to laugh or whine about my lack of career. His answer was always the same: Keep moving forward and don't look back. He was also an excellent tipper. So, yeah, I got an arrow to remind me of him and his advice. When people ask me what the arrow is for, I either give them the whole story, a short version, or sometimes I tell people it's where the tip goes. What I never do is cover it up and claim it's private. If I didn't want people to see it, it would not be where it is.

So, to the bartender with the private-symbol tattoo for all the world to see but for none of the world to understand, maybe you need to remember that making small talk is part of waiting tables and bartending. On the list of job expectations, "talking to people" falls right between "taking orders for food and drinks" and "wearing a polyester apron." It is also your responsibility to make sure that drunk-ass customers like me are not drinking so much that we dare to ask about so-called "private" tattoos that are clearly visible to everyone within three feet of you.

And speaking of being too inebriated to make good decisions, I also have a tattoo on my leg of Jiminy Cricket. If one of my customers were to see it and ask me what it means, I would proudly tell them, "Oh, I got that when I was twenty-one and in San Diego and had too much to drink. It means I make bad decisions when I'm drunk." That's called "small talk," and it's what servers do.

No Gluten? Sure, Ummm, Okay

Forgive me, Father, for I have sinned. I don't know if it's really a sin, but I may have done something to put someone in harm's way. Well, it wasn't really my fault, I guess, but I still feel bad about it, Lord. Okay, I don't really feel too bad about it because now that I think about it, it really didn't have much to do with me at all. Am I responsible for something I knew nothing about? Never mind, God, I'm sure she's fine.

All servers deal with customers who have allergies. It's part of our job to accommodate requests so that our guests can enjoy their food without worrying that their throats are going to swell up and they will get asphyxiated because they ate a nut. Of course I don't want someone to die because I forgot to type in "nut allergy" on the ticket. I can only assume that if you kill one of your customers, the tip is going to be pretty low, and you'll probably get a bad review online. I'm just going to assume . . .

I don't think gluten is ever going to kill anyone, but I don't want to be responsible for stomach cramps, either. There are a couple of regulars at the restaurant who can never eat gluten. One lady in particular is adamant about it, which I totally get. What I don't understand is how she can ask me every single time if the sauce that goes onto the roasted chicken is gluten-free.

"No, ma'am. The sauce has flour in it. We have not changed the recipe since the last time you were here, I'm sorry."

"Oh, really?" she says. "That's a bummer, because I'm allergic to gluten. Like, if I even have a little bit of it, I don't feel well. It's horrible for me. Like I even have to have my own mayonnaise at home because if my husband gets crumbs in the mayo and I use it, I get sick. Blech! Toilet for hours, you know what I mean? So, can you make sure the kitchen knows to be very careful? Thank you!"

"Yes, ma'am, absolutely."

"Okay, so I will have the roasted chicken with no sauce, okay? No sauce. Like not even on the side. I will regret it if I eat it. Thank you!"

"Yes, ma'am, very good."

Every time we go through this. Every. Single. Time. I got it, lady: You don't eat gluten. It gives you projectile diarrhea or whatever. Enough, already.

A few days later, the phone rings at work, and being the dutiful employee, I answer it on the seventh ring, since it seems clear that no one else is going to fucking do it.

"Thank you for calling. This is Darron. How may I help you?"

A lady on the other end wants to hear the specials of the day. I rattle them off and she decides she wants to place an order for pickup.

"This is what I get for answering the phone," I think. *"Now I have to ring this in under my number, and I know she isn't going to leave a tip on a to-go order. Where do we keep the to-go boxes, anyway? Fuck. I will never answer the phone again!"*

I place the order and rummage around the bar to find all the to-go utensils for a curry cauliflower soup and roasted chicken breast with no gravy. I think nothing about the order until fifteen minutes later, when the food is in the window. I put it all together and place it on top of the oven to keep it warm until the customer comes in to get it. The bartender will probably deal with it so I don't give it another thought.

A few minutes later, I notice that the food is gone, so I look over at the bar to see the bartender thanking the customer as she walks out the door with her soup and roasted chicken with no gravy. As she passes in front of our window I see that it is the "no-gluten" lady, and she is happily carrying a gluten-free roasted chicken and a cup of curry cauliflower soup that has gluten all up in it. Is she going to end up sitting on the toilet all night long, cursing my name? Should I run down the street to warn her about this toxic soup she ordered?

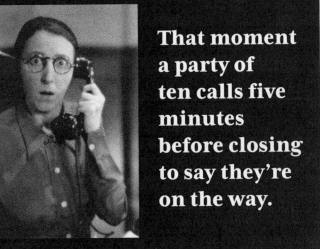

That moment a party of ten calls five minutes before closing to say they're on the way.

The Softer Side of Bitch

MAC AND CHEESE + CALAMARI = FRIENDSHIP

I sn't it funny how one tiny happening can immediately send your brain to something entirely different? A scent or a song seems to be the quickest route down memory lane. Whenever I smell a woman wearing rosewater perfume, I automatically think of two people—my Mamo Rita and my dear friend, Missi—because they both wore it. And I can't listen to the song "Cherish" without turning into a big ball of mushy tears because when I was about sixteen years old, my uncle transferred some silent home movies to video, and that's one of the songs he used for audio. Whenever I hear it, all I think of is the scratchy home-movie image of my dad, laughing on the floor and holding me when I was about one year old. These emotional assaults always take us by surprise, but they are always so welcome, and sometimes they happen while waiting tables.

One day, I take an order for calamari and go to the computer to ring it in, as I always do. I must be in a hurry, because I accidentally hit the button for macaroni and cheese instead. As soon as the ticket prints in the kitchen, I am there to tell the chef to ignore the "mac" and make a "mari" instead. About five minutes later, the chef puts the calamari in the window and says, "Hey, your mac-a-mari is ready!" I thank him, and when I pick up the plate, I realize he just said "Mac Amari." This is the name of one of my best friends in the whole world. Her initials in college were M. A. C., so we always called her "Mac." After she got married, her last name changed to Amari, so now she is Mac Amari. Of course, the chef has no idea he just yelled out the name of one of my favorite people in the world, someone I have known for over twenty-five years and don't get to see nearly often enough because we live so far away from each other. So there I am in the kitchen, holding a plate of calamari and suddenly overcome with emotion.

"Oh my God," I think. "I have not talked to her in forever." As Table 7 waits for their appetizer, I take a mental break and flash back to college, where I first met Mac. I think about the time we went shopping together and we both bought the same pair of pants and the same shirt but in different colors. Then we went back to her apartment to put on our nearly identical outfits and do a photo shoot. (Yeah, I bought ladies' pants. So what?)

I think about how, on my first Thanksgiving away from my family in 1985, she took me to her parents' house in Alamosa, Colorado. Her family embraced me and got me through the sadness of not being with my own family in Texas. I remember how she used to have a dry-erase board on her dorm-room door, and I wrote a poem on it that she liked so much that she kept it there all semester. Eventually, she typed it out on her typewriter and put it inside a photo collage that I still have.

Meanwhile, Table 7 is wondering what the hell happened to their appetizer.

I flash back to the time I had a layover in Denver just months after moving away from there. Mac and several others met me at the Denver airport, and we had a picnic at the gate before I got back on the plane and flew away from my best friends in the world. I remember how I spent my twenty-fourth birthday lying on her couch because I was sick, and she still made sure I had a wonderful celebration, surrounded by friends and a cake.

All of this comes from placing an order for mac and cheese instead of calamari, but I am happy that it happened. It reminds me that no matter what my job is, I have friends who make my life special. I have always felt lucky to have so many friends. There are people I met in the second grade I could call right now and talk to about anything. In those thirty seconds that it took for me to carry the calamari to Table 7, over two decades of friendship flashed before my eyes.

I put the plate down, and the customer says, "Thank you."

"No," I reply. "Thank you."

7 Tips to Keep in Mind When Waiting Tables

1. **DO NOT GET STRESSED OUT.** No matter how big of a hurry Table 7 is in, you have to remind yourself that there is no such thing as a lunch emergency. We can do our best to put the order in expeditiously and have their check ready when they need it, but no amount of pleading from customers is going to make that chicken breast cook any faster. Unless they want a side of salmonella, they are going to have to wait. If they are "desperate to get this meal in ten minutes," they shouldn't be in a damn restaurant.

2. **NEVER LET THEM SEE YOU SWEAT.** If you show your tables that you are weeded out beyond control, they are going to think that you can't handle your job—and sometimes that is the one crack that a cheap-ass needs to justify his 8 percent tip. If you remain calm, professional, and in control, and always do your very best, you will know that if and when you get a lousy tip, it's because the customer sucks at life and not because you suck as a server.

3. **LEARN THE NAMES OF THE BACK-OF-HOUSE CREW, AND BE NICE TO THEM.** Too many times, servers don't bother to get to know the dishwasher or all the prep guys in the kitchen. Sometimes, those are the people who can save your ass. Imagine this: It is a slammed Saturday night, and you just set down six desserts at your table, but you see there are no clean spoons. If you go to the dishwasher and scream at him to do his fucking job, do you think he is going to be inclined to move any faster for your sorry ass? No, he won't. However, if you have taken the time to get to know

him, and you can ask him, by name, to please rush some silver for you, he'll do it. Same thing with the guys behind the line. Oh, you forgot to ring in that well-done burger? Well, if you're friendly with the line cook, he'll do you a favor. (Hint: Always ask the kitchen crew if they need anything to drink, and then go get it for them. They'll love you for it.)

4. **ALWAYS BE HONEST WITH YOUR CUSTOMERS.** If you forget to ring in something, do not blame the kitchen or give the tired "Our printer went down" excuse. Customers will know you're lying, and your tip will suffer as a result. Tell them the truth, and they will appreciate it. I once served the president of the National Restaurant Association or some bullshit like that. (It was in my very short career in fine dining.) He asked me to recommend a bottle of wine. Since none of the bottles of wine on our menu came in a box, I wasn't sure what to say. I was also very new and my wine knowledge was weak. I almost made something up, but decided to be honest, instead. "Sir," I said. "I am very new here, and rather than making a poor recommendation, would you allow me to find a more experienced server to assist you in your decision?" He shook my hand and thanked me for my honesty. Then he gave me a 40 percent tip.

5. **YOU TAKE THE GOOD, YOU TAKE THE BAD.** Sometimes you will get a 25 percent tip, and sometimes you will get no tip at all. It all balances out in the end, and no amount of bitching is going to change it. (Yes, I recognize the irony of the "Bitchy Waiter" telling you not to bitch.) If customers leave you a bad tip, it is never worth it to chase them down and ask them what was wrong with the service. They aren't going to leave you more money, and you are just taking time away from your other tables, who will probably more than make up for it.

6. **BE THANKFUL THAT YOU DON'T HAVE TO TAKE YOUR JOB HOME WITH YOU.** If you find yourself getting stressed out, just remember that when your shift ends, so does your responsibility. You're not on call, and other than the occasional server nightmare or slight whiff of fajita smoke in your hair, you won't even think about your job when you're not there. It's one of the things that gets me through my shift sometimes.

7. **SHIFT DRINKS.** Enough said.

Another Server Nightmare

It is 4:36 a.m., and I have been jolted out of bed by the fury that is a server's nightmare. I try to go back to sleep, but every time I close my eyes, I am right back in the same moment of the dream that had woken me up in the first place. It is horrible. I know it was only a dream, but it seemed so real. My mattress is a puddle of sweat and angst, and my covers are rolled into a ball at the foot of the bed. I reach over to take a sip of the vodka I keep on my bedside table, but the glass is drier than my throat. I am forced to get up and head to the liquor cabinet to quench my thirst. Once up, I have no choice but to sit at the computer and relay this horror story in the hopes that, by retelling it, I can exorcise it from my body.

In the dream, I am working at a hotel again, as I did for 6½ years of my server life. It is a broken-down, tired-as-hell hotel that has seen better days. I am filling in for someone as a favor and have never been to this property before. It is the breakfast shift, and I am already in a bad mood just because of what time it is. When I arrive at the restaurant, I learn that I am the only one on the floor with no other servers and no support staff. There is no sidework sheet telling me what needs to be done, so I begin doing what I know how to do. After I determine where all the lights are, so I can see what I am doing, I begin to make coffee. As soon as I find the filters, a customer appears and seats himself.

"Excuse me?" he yells across the dining room. "I need two hard-boiled eggs and dry rye toast. I'm in a hurry because I have a meeting. And some coffee would be nice."

"Yes, sir, I am making some right now."

This is when I realize that every bag of coffee I pick up is decaf, and no one wants decaf in the morning. I go to the computer to place his order and can see into the kitchen, which has no lights on and is completely vacant. I can also see the man watching me to make sure I place his order so I ring it in, knowing full well that no cook will see it when it comes out of the printer.

"Hello? Coffee?" I hear the man say.

I go to pour his decaf and I see that there are three other people who are waiting to be seated. None of the tables have been set with silverware or jellies or butters or creams, but I take them to the nearest booth. They, too, are in a hurry.

The restaurant is connected to the front desk of the hotel in that weird way dreams have of merging two different places into one. I can see that even though there is no one at the front desk, there is a couple waiting to speak with someone. They flag me down to check them into their room, but I tell them that I will find someone else to help them. Of course, there is no phone for me to use.

"Can I get more coffee? And I need my hard-boiled eggs."

"We need menus."

"Can we get a table?" Inexplicably, there is another group of people waiting to be seated.

This is when I wake up. I am safe and sound in my bed—sweaty, but okay. I lay my head back on the pillow to go back to sleep to dream of nicer things, like waterslides of chocolate pudding and couches made of nachos. As soon as I am asleep, though, I am back at the infernal hotel.

"Excuse us, we have been waiting for a table for two minutes. Is anyone going to help us? Do you even want our business or not?"

I tell them to sit wherever they'd like, and I will be with them right away. Thankfully, I notice that someone has appeared at the front desk, so at least I don't have to worry about that anymore. The woman at the front desk is a tall, icy blond with her hair pulled back in a tight bun and a small scarf tied around her neck, looking like a reject from a flight attendant fashion show.

The restaurant has shifted shape again, and now I notice a set of French doors next to the sidestand. Through the doors I see a white limousine coming to a stop right outside the hotel. I watch the driver get out and walk around the car to open the door for the passenger, Jesse Tyler Ferguson from the television show *Modern Family*. He is wearing a natty bow tie and suit, and he's heading right toward me.

"Hello. I'm having an event here for my charity and the rest of the guests should be here in about ten minutes—about 150 to 200. Where should we go?"

I am dumbfounded. By now the restaurant has filled up, and I still have only taken one order for two hard-boiled eggs that was sent to a kitchen without any cooks in it. I have one pot of decaf made, the tables are still not set, and I can't find any menus.

That moment you're at home and remember you never took those extra lemons to Table 16.

"So where should we go?" asks Jesse Tyler Ferguson once more.

"I love your bow tie. Would you like some coffee?" I ask him.

"Only if it's decaf."

Overjoyed that I can finally give someone something he asked for, I rush over to the coffeepot to pour him a cup. Standing there, I see six-time Tony Award–winner Audra McDonald.

"Hey," she says. "I noticed that you made decaf. Nobody wants decaf in the morning, so I dumped it out and found the regular and just made you a new pot. You're welcome. I love your hair."

"What are you doing here?" I say.

"Oh, you just seemed like you needed some help, *so here I am!*" She says those last three words the same way she does when she sings "Mister Snow" from *Carousel*.

I love Audra McDonald so much that I can't tell her that I needed that decaf, so I take a cup of regular to Jesse Tyler Ferguson and hope for the best. When I get to him, he is surrounded by a mob of people, including Angela Lansbury, Anjelica Huston, my friend Lisa from the second grade, and Puck from the 1994 cast of *The Real World*.

"My friends are here. Where should we go? We're in a hurry."

"I need more coffee, and where are my eggs?"

"We need menus!"

"Can we order?"

"We need a table!"

The restaurant is overflowing with people. I am about to break down from the stress. I am alone and fearful and in need of a drink. I don't know what to do, so I run to the dark kitchen and hide in the walk-in.

This is when I wake up again. I am too scared to go back to sleep. I don't want to go back to that nightmare and see the disappointment in Jesse Tyler Ferguson's face when he learns I gave him regular coffee. I can't bear to have Audra McDonald see me again while I am dressed in a polyester maroon vest. So now I sit at the computer, hoping that if I stay up long enough, the horrific server nightmare will fade away into the deep recesses of my brain.

CHAPTER SIX

THE RESTAURANT THAT SHALL NOT BE NAMED

THERE ARE THOUSANDS OF RESTAURANTS IN New York City, and I have worked at most of them. I had the unfortunate experience of working at one particular upscale, celebrity chef–owned restaurant for all of three weeks. (I was let go because of "scheduling issues," but I'm pretty sure that's not the real reason.) One day after my firing, the restaurant instituted a social media policy about blogging. You're welcome, Restaurant That Shall Not Be Named.

I Got a New Job

Do you hear the angels singing? Do you see the rainbow forming in the sky and ending at my doorstep with a unicorn sliding down it? Do you get a whiff of the sweet smell of success? I started a new job. (Cue confetti cannons and balloons, please.) I begin training with what we all know and love: trailing. For those of you not in the know, "trailing" is when a new server follows behind someone who shows him the ropes. I hate it. Give me a table chart and a menu, and tell me how to ring in food, and I'm good to go. It's especially annoying when the one who is training me has been on the earth for a shorter period of time than the Smiths concert T-shirt that I sleep in. But what choice do I have? None. Like a helpless puppy, I follow Mike around so he can tell me where the salt is kept in dry storage and where the dirty linens go after being removed from the tables. Important, yes, but there are so many other things that I want to know on my first day of work. Unfortunately, I just can't blurt these things out:

- What do we get for shift meal, and when is it?

- How much did you walk away with in tips yesterday?

- Which of the managers are bitches, and which ones are cool?

- Are we really not supposed to use our cell phones, or is that just something they say to the new people? Because I saw that girl texting in the sidestand.

- The manager said that our jeans have to be a certain shade, so I went out and bought a new pair, but now I see people all over the place with faded ones. What the hell?

- Is the chef who is expediting always so cunty?

- Which of the servers are not cool? I don't want to waste time getting to know them if they are losers.

- Do Jay Z and Beyoncé really come in here all the time, or is that something they say at the orientation so I'll be all excited about my new place of employment?

- Are the managers gonna have an issue with me needing to be off November 15-17? Because I kinda want to go to Washington, D.C. for a couple of days.

- It's great that we have a barista who deals with all the coffees, teas, and cappuccinos, but how much am I going to be tipping his ass out?

- Do I really have to use a tray to carry a single glass of water? Because that is so dumb.

- What happens if I fail my menu quiz? Do I really need to memorize every fucking ingredient in the chicken liver-toast appetizer?

- Which hostess is the biggest whore? I just wanna know.

I suppose I'll eventually figure out all these things. It's hard being the new guy. None of them know how totally cool I am yet. It took me long enough to find this goddamn job, and, soon, some of them will do something that warrants a story about them. But will they know about it? Hell, no. This is my secret.

Holly Has a Lemon Up Her Ass

You know the old saying that you never get a second chance to make a first impression? Well, such is the case with a couple of people at Restaurant That Shall Not Be Named. I have a manager I shall refer to as Holly, who has made a very strong first impression on my first day at the job. And that impression is one I would suspect she'd like to have a second chance at.

It is my first shift meeting, and I am getting bombarded with all kinds of information that either I don't understand or feel is unnecessary to know. And then Holly has something to say. Let me paint a picture of her, so you can imagine what I have to look at. She wears glasses on the tip of her nose—all the better to peer over them in a condescending manner—and she must have a lemon up her ass, because her face is in constant sourpuss mode. You know what they say: When life gives you lemons, you shove them up your asshole.

"Okay," says Holly. "So, during opening sidework this morning, someone thought they would put their personal music into our system. That is not acceptable. The music that is played in the restaurant also plays in the mezzanine of our neighboring store." (We share a space with a fancy retail store.) "Not okay."

Then another manager (I'll call him Lispy) says, "Yeth. Now at night I thimply don't thay anything becauth the sthore ith clothed. But during the day, we abtholutely cannot do that."

Now my thought is this: If you allow it at night and have never told anyone that it is not all right to do the same thing during the day, how in hell is anyone supposed to know that? Holly then pulls the MP3 player from her crocheted vest pocket and asks to whom it belongs. A server

manager (noun): **A person who holds papers and looks concerned in an effort to appear important or in charge.**

raises his hand and apologizes. "Don't let it happen again," she hisses, and she tosses it across the bar, letting it bounce a few times before coming to rest in front of the vilified server. Is there any reason for her to fling it across the room? It was an honest mistake, and she could have broken the fucking device just because she wants to throw her authority around. All the servers inhale a collective "oooh" when it hits the bar. Holly pushes her glasses back up her nose and then readjusts herself on her barstool, presumably to see if it is time for the lemon to come out of her ass. It isn't time, and it will never be time. That lemon is there for eternity.

What is my first impression of Holly? She is an overly dramatic ice queen bitch who takes any opportunity to remind people that she is boss.

Dear Bitchy,

I work in a fine-dining restaurant in a major city. My boss is always telling me that I come off as arrogant to my coworkers. He says that I like to make people believe that I am smarter than they are. How do I make him understand that this isn't really my intention; it's just that I am smarter than everyone else, and it's just way too easy to show it? Should I dumb myself down? Should I pretend that I am a completely uneducated redneck in order to make my coworkers feel better about themselves? Please help!

Signed,

S. B.

Dear S. B.,

So, you are smarter than everyone around you, and people think you are arrogant because of it? I don't see the problem here. In no way should you dumb yourself down to make your coworkers feel better about themselves. Are these coworkers people you care about or spend time with outside of work? Do any of them have anything to do with your life, other than sharing a computer and tray jacks? If the answer to these questions is no, then who gives a fuck, sweetie? I say turn your diploma into a necklace and wear that bitch around your neck, or have it printed onto fabric and then turn it into an apron. If your coworkers are all as dumb as a bag of hair, it's their issue and not yours. How about you purchase an "I'm with Stupid" T-shirt? You could wear it underneath your uniform, and whenever someone accuses you of being arrogant, simply unbutton enough of your shirt to reveal your innermost thoughts.

Of course, if it will make everyone around you feel better, you could bring your intelligence down a few pegs. When someone asks if you did your sidework, you can ask her, "Which side?" Or when the kitchen staff tells you that the spinach artichoke dip is 86'ed, tell them that Table 12 wanted the dip, and you don't even have a Table 86. Duh. If you want people to think you are stupid, volunteer to pick up a couple of hostess *shifts—that ought to do it. The number one way you can make people at your job question your intelligence, though, is to tell them that you asked for advice from me. Once they find that out, it would go something like this:*

WAITER: *Man, that S.B. thinks she is so smart. She was telling me she watched the Republican presidential debate last night.*

WAITRESS: *Like that makes her smart. God, I hate her.*

WAITER: *And then I saw her doing a crossword puzzle.*

WAITRESS: *What an arrogant bitch. Why doesn't she just do a word search like everyone else?*

WAITER: *I know, right? And she doesn't use a calculator when she does her paperwork.*

WAITRESS: *What a fucking show-off!*

WAITER: *And she was telling me she liked one of the Bitchy Waiter's blog posts.*

WAITRESS: *Wait, she reads the Bitchy Waiter? Maybe she's not as smart as we thought.*

S.B., I hope this helps. I say embrace your big fat brain and make everyone at your job feel stupid around you. If they are stupid, it's not your fault. So go out there and quote some Friedrich Nietzsche and carry around War and Peace. *That way, when they are discussing the most recent episode of* The Real Housewives *and talking about the latest issue of* Star *magazine, you can rest assured that your $200,000 college education wasn't a complete waste of money.*

Mustard and mayo,

The Bitchy Waiter

Two Bitches Are Better Than One

In my continuing series of first impressions of the people at my new job, let me focus my attention on another manager I shall refer to as Krystle. Not because she looks like the pristine flower Krystle Carrington from the hit television show of the 1980s, *Dynasty*, but because I always wanted a poodle named Krystle Carrington—and this lady might be as close as I ever get to having one, with her curly hair and uppity attitude. On my second day at work, I am standing near the bar when I feel a tap on my shoulder.

"Hi, I'm Krystle and I'm a manager. I need you *[pause]* to tuck your shirt in."

I quickly apologize and do as I am told, only to look up and see that she has vanished. Really? That's how she's going to introduce herself to a new employee? I have seen her for two days already and thought she was a hostess because she has never said one word to me. And before you think I was being slobby or disrespectful about leaving my shirttails untucked, let me inform you that I reached that decision very carefully. I noticed that most of the women did not have their shirts tucked in, and none of the bartenders did, including the guys. Anyway, my shirt always comes untucked whenever I reach up to a high shelf, bend over to pick up some crap off the floor, or fall to my knees, asking, "Why God? Why? Why didn't I want to grow up to be a doctor?"

Krystle has nothing else to say to me on this day, but I watch her. And I question why it was *me* who had to have his shirt tucked in? And who is *she* to make that style-based decision? This chick has a nose ring, a lip piercing, black stretch pants, tacky-ass boots, and a fur vest. And it's my *shirt* that is inappropriate? Okay, Krystle.

As the days pass, Krystle says very little to me. On one occasion, I have to discuss my schedule with her because she completely ignored the fact that I told them I could only work part-time because of another job and my life. She scheduled me all through the week, with conflicts up the wazoo. She tells me to email her and that she will take care of it.

"I will *not* be there on Tuesday, Krystle." the email says. Thirty-six hours after I sent the email, and still no response.

The only other time she approaches me is when I accidentally shut a cabinet door too hard, and it makes a banging sound. She rushes over to me and tells me I need to be quieter. Keep in mind it is 9:00 on a Saturday night, we are packed with customers, and I can barely hear myself think. If she thinks the door is disturbingly loud, she might want to hop over to the ten-top at Table 14 who are on their fifth bottle of wine and ask them to bring it down a decibel or two. (Also, I am probably old enough to be her father, and I kinda hate her for that reason alone.) I want to send some Alexis Carrington Colby over to this woman, so she can kick her ass in a lily pond.

More days go by, and she fails to respond to the email letting her know that I will not be at work on Tuesday. I have made the decision that no news is good news and assume everything will be fine.

·ᴄᵔᴖᴏ·

My other manager I will call Porcelain Doll because she is always so put-together and pristine that if she smiles, her fucking face will crack apart. Not surprisingly, she's a bitch. The first day I see her, she forces a weak smile and extends her tiny, wimpy hand out for me to shake as she introduces herself.

At least she tried to smile, I think. Her grip is that of a wet soba noodle. The next time I see her, I am trying to ring in an order without the assistance of a trainer, and she is standing next to the computer.

"Oh, Porcelain Doll, I'm glad you're here. Would you please make sure I am ringing in this order the right way before I send it to the kitchen?"

"Well, I'm not just *standing* here because you're pretty," says Porcelain Doll.

Wait, is she being funny or being a bitch? I pat my naturally curly hair and say, "Well, thank you for calling me pretty," and then produce a little girly laugh. Porcelain Doll doesn't move her face, and it is clear that she isn't being funny. What is it with these managers? Are they required to take an aptitude test to determine that none of them have a funny bone in their body? Do any of them understand what a sense of humor is? Can't any of them see that what they do is not as important as what a brain surgeon or the secretary of defense does? I have repeatedly tried to lighten things up around here, only to be shot back down by a no-nonsense stare from a pair of glassed-over eyes. Porcelain Doll seems to be the worst one when it comes to having any fun. She needs to be put under glass and displayed at the Museum for Artifacts of Lame Shit. Admission would be a suggested donation of $5, but no one would ever pay that amount to get in because the only people who would go there would be kids who have to write a report on it for their social studies class. Porcelain Doll would just sit there and wait for someone to look at her before she eventually dried up and deteriorated into a pile of dust that the janitor would vacuum up and toss into a dumpster. A perfect ending for a perfect bitch.

Can You Hear Me Now?

At this new job, there is absolutely no communication between management and staff. All the managers have their heads so far up their asses that they must not have any signal on their smartphones, because they never respond to emails, even though I was initially told that "Email is the best way for us to all stay connected." Email is only as good as the person who opens the fucking emails, idiots.

The schedule is still full of conflicts for me because no one ever bothers to ask about my life. At the first interview I told Holly about my other job and that I could only work certain days.

"Sure. No problem. We love people who are willing to take only a few shifts a week, so that maybe they'll be able to pick up extra shifts when we need it."

Clearly, she did not know whom she was talking to. Me pick up extra shifts? That's funny, Holly. At the first day of orientation, they gave us the spiel about our required five days of training, and after we had completed those, they would let us know if we would be invited to stay on as a member of the team. (Finally, I could be on a *team*. Take that, all you assholes from junior high who chose me last for kickball.) I assumed that they would also speak to us about our availability at that point, since they have a set schedule and I have a life outside their restaurant. That didn't happen. Krystle posted the schedule willy-nilly with me all over the place.

After a couple of attempts at getting in touch with her, she finally emails me back, saying she will send out an email to get the shift covered and "no worries." Great, I do not have to worry about it, then. But of

clopening: When you close the restaurant one night and open it the next morning.

course there will be a communication breakdown, and whichever manager is working on Tuesday will have no idea why I haven't shown up.

I am supposed to be there at noon. At 12:15, my cell phone rings, which I don't answer because I am in the shower. Thirty seconds later the landline phone rings, and this is what I hear from the bathroom:

"Uh, hi, Darron? Thith ith Lithpy? And I thee that you're on the thhedule for today? But I don't thee you here? Tho can you call me ath thoon ath you get thith methage? Thankth."

I cannot stand how he and the other managers all talk as if everything is a question. I want to find a period, stuff it in his mouth, and cram the perpetual question mark up his asshole. I *knew* this would happen. Krystle didn't find someone to cover my shift for me, as she said she would, and now I look like the new employee who doesn't take his new job seriously. I did not plan on letting it be that obvious for at least three more weeks.

I call back and speak to whichever hostess picks up the phone. Lispy is busy, so she tells me she will pass on my information, and he will call me back if he needs to talk to me. He doesn't call back because I had read the email to the hostess that Krystle sent to me, saying that she was taking care of it.

Later that day, I receive an email that went out to the entire staff about shift coverage and the correct procedure. I know that it was sent on my behalf. And you know what? I won't be there on Sunday, either, for the same reason: I have another job, I told them I did, they said it was okay, and Krystle said she'd take care of it.

All Bad Things Must Come to an End

I have now been at Restaurant That Shall Not Be Named for three weeks. It is coming to the end of my lunch shift, and all seems to be going okay. As I am resetting the last of my tables and preparing to do my final pieces of sidework, Lispy sashays over to me.

"Ummm, Darron? When you're finithed with that table, can you pleath come downstairth to thee me in my offith?"

"Oh, sure. I just have to get some plates from the dish room to restock the cabinet first and then I'll be right there."

"Acthually, juth come right now," he counters.

"Oh, am I finally getting my ID card so security will let me into the building without the third degree?" I ask.

"Follow me."

I walk behind him through the kitchen, into the hallway, down the stairs, and into his office, where he asks me to sit down. He sits at his desk and puts both his elbows on it, resting his chin on the back of his raised hands.

"Tho, you're a cool guy and everything? But, ummm, I think we are going to have to athk you to leave uth at thith time?"

I feign surprise. "Are you firing me? I don't understand. I thought I was doing a good job here."

"Yeth, um, don't get me wrong? You're a cool guy, but we don't theem to think you are gelling with everyone here and we need thomeone who hath more availability to be on the thchedule? Tho, yeah."

My mind is racing because I have never been fired in my life.

"When I applied, you knew I had a second job, and you were fine with me working here part time. Has something changed in three weeks?"

"I mean, you're a cool guy and everything . . . You jutht have too many thcheduling ithues?"

I am relieved this is happening because this job has been nothing but miserable for me. The staff is rude, the management is uncommunicative, the hours are long, most of the customers are self-entitled whine bags, and—most of all—the tip pool is a mockery that was never explained to me. On one night, my sales were $2,500. I kept track of my tips and made about $500—$411 in credit cards tips and $90 in cash, which went to a bartender for safekeeping. Their formula for tipping out is a point-based system that calculates who gets what percentage of all of the tips made the entire night. The total of the tips are tallied and then it trickles down to servers, back servers, bartenders, bar-backs, food runners, hosts, the people in the back who make the coffee, and a partridge in a pear tree. After all of that, my take-home was about $175 for that night, or only 35 percent of what I had made.

"So, I'm being fired for 'scheduling issues,' is that it?" I confirm.

Lispy nods his head, which I take to mean that he is agreeing with me, but it could be that he is bouncing his head to a show tune that only he can hear.

"Okay," I say. "I'll be on my way then. I guess I can come in next week to pick up my last check and the tips from today. Is that all right?"

His head continues to bob up and down, and I can almost hear the strains of *Hello Dolly's* "Before the Parade Passes By" echoing in his skull. I hand in my apron and head to my locker to empty it out. I see other servers looking at me and wonder how many of them know why I am being fired. I leave Restaurant That Shall Not Be Named and feel lighter than I have in weeks. As soon as I get home, I reopen my unemployment claim and start looking for a new job.

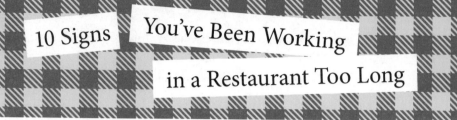

10 Signs You've Been Working in a Restaurant Too Long

1. **YOU CATCH YOURSELF SAYING "BEHIND YOU" TO TOTAL STRANGERS.** It's happened to all of us at one time or another. There is an old lady in the produce aisle at the grocery store, and she is moving slower than a snail covered in molasses in January. As you squeeze past her, those words fall out of your mouth, and you wish you could rewind. If the salad dressing stains on your shirt didn't already tell her you work in a restaurant, your words just did.

2. **YOU WON'T WEAR BLACK PANTS OR A BLACK SHIRT ANYWHERE BECAUSE IT MAKES YOU FEEL LIKE YOU ARE GOING TO WORK.** Or khakis with a Polo shirt. And anytime you see people wearing all black at an event, you know they have never worked as a cater waiter before. If you wear all black to a catered event, someone is inevitably going to ask you where the restroom is.

3. **WHEN YOU GO INTO A RESTAURANT, THE FIRST THING YOU DO IS WONDER HOW MUCH THE WAITER IS "WALKING WITH" AFTER THE SHIFT.** I once saw an interview with Edie Falco, who waited tables for years in New York City before hitting it big on *The Sopranos*. She said that she still can't pass a restaurant without wondering what it's like to work there and, if they're hiring, how good the tips are.

4. **YOU WON'T GO INTO A RESTAURANT UNLESS IT IS OPEN FOR AT LEAST ONE MORE HOUR.** Servers probably over-compensate for this. Most people feel okay going in with thirty minutes or even fifteen minutes left until closing. I need an hour to feel comfortable.

5. **YOU HAVE CONSIDERED HOW HANDY IT WOULD BE TO WEAR AN APRON OUTSIDE OF WORK BECAUSE THOSE DARN POCKETS ARE FREAKIN' USEFUL.** Let's face it: When you are at the Laundromat, you wish you had on an apron to reach into and pull out your quarters and the dryer sheet. And have you ever been somewhere and needed a pen, so you instinctively reached down to where your apron would be to grab one?

6. **YOU HOARD PENS.** Customers steal pens and so do your coworkers. You never have enough, which is why every time you walk by a TD Bank®, you stop in and grab a handful. It's not stealing; it's advertising.

7. **YOU THINK YOUR HAIR IS SUPPOSED TO SMELL THAT WAY.** It's not. It should smell like shampoo, not honey mustard or crushed dreams.

8. **WHEN DINING OUT, YOU TELL YOUR SERVER "THANK YOU" ABOUT THREE DOZEN TIMES.** You may also use the phrases "whenever you get a chance," "if you don't mind," and "I'm sorry to bother you, but . . ."

9. **IF YOU USE KETCHUP AT A RESTAURANT, THE FIRST THING YOU DO IS LOOK AT THE INSIDE OF THE CAP TO SEE IF THE SERVER DID HIS SIDEWORK.** We all hate cleaning ketchup lids, but we do it because nothing is more disgusting than opening up a ketchup bottle and seeing a scab of week-old ketchup encrusted around the edge.

10. **YOU WRITE A BOOK ABOUT IT.** Enough said.

The Softer Side of Bitch

RITA ON THE ROCKS, NO SALT

Whenever I take an order for a margarita and write it down on my pad, it makes me smile. Not just because I worship all things tequila, but because Rita is the name of my grandmother. I told her once that every time I take an order for a margarita, I write down her name because that is the abbreviation servers use. She thought that was the funniest thing. "Yeah," I told her. "Sometimes I write down your name ten or fifteen times in one day."

My mamo was one cool lady. She was born in 1922, and she had her own dress shop sometime in the early 1960s. I have a picture of her leaning against the sign that says RITA'S DRESS SHOPPE. Her hair is dark and wavy, and she is shielding her eyes from the sun.

I have a lot of restaurant memories with Mamo. She and my papo used to take me and my brothers to Kips Big Boy every time we went to see them in Houston. It's funny that I don't remember what I ate, but I remember how excited we were to go there. When we got out of the car, the first thing we would do was run over to the statue of Kip that stood in front of the restaurant. We always had our picture taken in front of it, and damned if I know where one single copy of any of those pictures are now. When I was at her house, it was like my own little Mexican restaurant. She would make whatever I wanted, and I always wanted the same thing: tortillas. I would sit in the kitchen and marvel at how quickly she could make them from scratch, rolling them out into a perfect circle and throwing them onto the skillet. She never used tongs to flip them—just her hands. She would reach into the pan and grab the edge of the tortilla to flip it, and when it was done she would toss it onto a plate covered with a used piece of aluminum foil that she had pulled from her drawer. Sometimes she would make refried beans or a scrambled egg to go with them, or maybe I would just eat them with butter and sugar.

"Aye, m'hijo, how can you eat so many tortillas?" she would wonder out loud. I could eat as many as she could make. "Aye, m'hijo, you put too much salt on your eggs; your blood pressure is going to go up. No salt. No salt."

I loved salt, and I would add more to my eggs just because it was funny to see her get so exasperated over a few sprinkles. She tried to teach me how to make tortillas once, when I was about nineteen. Of course she didn't have a recipe, so it was "about this much" and "about that much," and when I tried to make them on my own, they were a colossal failure. I couldn't even get them to be round.

Another food memory I have of Mamo is how she always had ice cream sandwiches in her freezer. When I stayed with her, I loved to swim in the pool of her apartment complex and then come into the air-conditioning and watch cartoons while eating ice cream sandwiches.

"Can I have another one, Mamo?"

"If you want another one, you go right ahead," she'd say. "But aren't you cold? How can you be all wet and eat ice cream?"

I'd run to the freezer to grab another one and plop down on my stomach, resting my head on my elbows.

"Aye, m'hijo, don't eat like that. You can't digest your food if you're on your belly. Roll over." I'd roll my eyes, and then I'd roll over.

Is your grandma still alive? Call her. Say hello. Ask her a question that only she will have the answer to. *What was it like to live through the Great Depression? Why did you always name your Chihuahuas "Peanut"?* I talked to Mamo Rita all the time. I could tell her anything at all, and she would tell me things, too. I didn't want to hear about her sex life after my papo died, but she told me anyway. We would talk about *Survivor* and *American Idol* and the weather. Every New Year's Eve, I would call her at midnight because she loved that moment when we all looked to the future, filled with hope.

I'm sad that she's gone but grateful that she had eighty-eight years of a good life. A long, happy marriage, kids, grandkids, travels . . . She used to get a new car every year because my papo treated her like a queen. No one loved Mamo more than Papo did. Every time I go to Texas and pass the Dairy Treet, I stop and get a burger in her honor, since it was her favorite fast food joint. And for as long as I am a waiter, every time someone orders a margarita, I will think of Mamo as I write down her name.

CHAPTER SEVEN

RESTAURANT REVERIES

WHEN YOU HAVE BEEN WAITING TABLES FOR as long as I have, sometimes you have to find ways to make it to the end of the shift. Very often, I let my mind wander and go on automatic-pilot mode, imagining myself in a completely different environment. I look at customers and create stories about how they might be outside the restaurant. On occasion, my mind wanders so far out of the realm of possibility that it takes me someplace far, far away from my apron and pad.

The Passion in Her Touch

I was fondled at work this week. Well, sort of. Let us look at this story as a creative writing exercise. I will begin with the story exactly as it happened, and at some point I will switch it to complete fiction. See if you can tell when it changes from storytelling to a big fat fucking bullshit lie.

It is a dark and stormy night on Sunday. The north wind is blowing, and the temperature has dropped to a chilly forty-five degrees, forcing me to use my hoodie to buffer the wind as I make my way to the club. I punch in and get ready for a three-show night.

"It's gonna be a tough night," I say to no one in particular as I wipe down tables and prepare the candles.

The first show is a jazz singer who is ready to wail and blow the roof off the joint. Her audience is light but enthusiastic. I take the drink orders before the show starts and ring them in, ready to serve my guests and give them a night that is perfectly enjoyable from all angles. (No, that is not where the story veers into fiction.) There is a broad at Table 28 who is also a trumpet player for the show. She only has to perform in two numbers, so she is sitting with her husband and having a glass of Cabernet as she waits for her time to get onstage. About halfway through the show, I begin clearing empty glasses and make room for the second rounds.

As I approach Table 28 for the lady's wineglass, she is facing the stage and cannot see that I am standing behind her and trying to clear her table. Surreptitiously, I reach my arm around her to pick up the glass when her hand reaches out to grab mine. Apparently, she thinks my hand is the hand of her husband. She holds it for a brief second as she continues to watch the stage. Pulling my hand away, I glance at the husband, who smiles at me, seeing what is happening and knowing that his wife thinks that my hand is his.

A spark ignites between his wife and my cold, cold heart. I reach back out to touch her hand again, and I feel the warmth of our passion flow from my fingertips to the innermost recesses of my soul and thaw out my heart that has been longing for this feeling for oh-so-many years. She

turns her head to look at her husband and realizes that it is not his hand she is caressing, but *mine*. Her cheeks flush with embarrassment, but then a sly smile comes across her face, making her lips a fuller, deeper red than I have ever seen on any woman before or since. She pulls her hand away and mutters, "Excuse me. I must go to the ladies' room." Racing toward the back of the room with her long, dark hair billowing behind her, I hear a sob escape from her throat that I recognize as regret filled with longing. I clear her wineglass and avoid eye contact with the husband.

Two minutes later, with everyone's attention fixed on the performance in the darkened room, I sneak over to the ladies' room and gently crack open the door. I see her leaning against the counter with her head hanging over the sink. Startled, she jerks her head to look at me, her eyes full of confusion and desire.

"It's okay," I say. "I feel the same way as you do."

She pulls me toward her and plants her full, moist lips on my mine, running her fingers through my hair. Kissing wildly, I am transported to a place where drink orders no longer matter and I am attracted to middle-aged female trumpet players. Her hand moves from my hair to the nape of my neck, to the small of my back. When our lips part, I look into her eyes, and a single tear falls down her cheek.

"My husband is . . ."

"I don't care about your husband," I say. "I am in love with you. Ever since your hand accidentally touched mine four minutes ago when I was bussing your table, nothing else in the world matters to me anymore."

I glance at the mirror behind her and see the reflection of her husband, staring back at me with a dark and steely gaze. I turn around to defend my love of his trumpet-playing, middle-aged wife. He rushes toward me, hands outreached, and I prepare to feel his fingers throttling my throat. Instead, he brushes the hair out of my eyes with his left thumb and puts his right hand on the nape of my neck, where his wife's hand had been only moments before. He pulls me close and kisses me with all the conviction he can muster. I struggle to get away but finally give in to his power. His wife then caresses me from behind, and a storm of kisses from husband and wife covers my neck, face, and lips.

Two minutes later, they are gone. I am alone in the women's bathroom, wondering what has just happened. I splash cold water on my face, straighten my apron, and go back to the bar. I carry out the second drinks, and my night goes on as usual. But I am forever changed.

WHAT INSPIRED THIS STORY: *A slow night at work when I needed anything to distract me from the fact that I wasn't going to make any money.*

Come and Knock on Our Door

Tuesday, March 15, 1977. Tonight was so slow at work. I have *got* to get a new job. It's bad enough that no one ever comes into the bar, but that uniform they make me wear is ridiculous. The stupid red skirt that's way too short and the puffy sleeves, with my tits on full display? C'mon. And then I have to wear that dumb-ass vest and apron and floppy hat? I look like I'm about to go milk Betsy Ross's cow. Oh, well. Maybe I'll be discovered some day. It *is* Hollywood, after all. (Okay, it's Santa Monica, but close enough.) Pretty much the only people who came in tonight were those losers from the apartment complex down the street—those two girls and that guy who all live together. But they all came in at different times, and they sat at three different tables.

First, the dumb blonde came in with a date. He must have been a doctor because he was wearing his scrubs, but I never trust a doctor who wears his scrubs in public. He seemed like a total lech who kept trying to make out with her, even though she kept saying no. Well, a few minutes later the dark-haired roommate showed up. I think she works at that broken-down flower shop up the street that always only has carnations and baby's breath in it. So she showed up, but she was in a trench coat and a hat, like she didn't want anyone to know who she was. Ummm, hello? You come in here every night, I recognize you, dumb ass. She sat down at the booth next to Dumb Blonde and started spying on them. She ordered water. Wow, thanks for coming in—that's really going to help me pay my rent. A few minutes later the guy roommate came in, and he was wearing a trench coat, too. He was trying to be all sneaky, but the first thing he did when he walked in was bump into that big potted plant we have by the door, knocking it over. He fell down, rolled halfway across the bar, and then jumped up like nothing happened and sat down at a table. What an idiot. He was wearing sunglasses. Uh, maybe *that's* why you didn't see the big fucking plant, dumb ass. He ordered a water, too. What a great night this was turning out to be.

So the two trench coat people just watched their friend on the date. Meanwhile, Dr. Lech was getting really fresh with Dumb Blonde. I don't know why she didn't just get up and leave. He ordered her another wine spritzer and tried to get her to drink it really fast.

A few minutes later, that old creepy married couple came in. His name is Stanley. I only know that because his wife says it over and over again. I don't know what her name is. I just call her Lady Who Wears Ugly Muumuus. She ordered a piña colada, and I had to tell her we don't have them. Again. She orders it every fucking time she comes in. Stanley ordered a beer. They sat at the bar, and she was hanging all over him, practically begging for some attention. He just ignored her. She eventually gave up and played darts by herself.

Meanwhile, Dr. Handsy was taking it too far with Dumb Blonde. That's when the two trench-coated losers got up to help their friend. And then they saw each other for the first time. They were all like, "What

SHOW ME A HAPPY WAITRESS AND I'LL SHOW YOU A DRUNK ONE.

are *you* doing here?" even though there was nobody else in the whole goddamn bar. They were arguing about how they were each there to protect Dumb Blonde (Chrissy, they said), and then they got mad at each other because I guess they had both promised Chrissy they wouldn't watch over her and they had both broken their promises. The next thing I know, Chrissy has dumped a pitcher of water on her date and told him to get out. Great, now I get to mop it all up. The "doctor" scurried out, and then Chrissy saw her roommates. She was all like, "What are *you* doing here?" and that's when I went to the bar and poured myself a shot of whiskey. Suddenly, they're all hugging and saying what great friends they are and laughing. I think they're on drugs or something. And then they see the older couple all of a sudden, and it turns out they know them, too. How they didn't see them earlier, I'll never know. Again, let me remind you, *they were the only people in the bar tonight.*

And then they all started to leave together. I had to grab them to make them pay their bills. Three wine spritzers for Chrissy and one beer for Stanley. They each left me a dollar. Fucking assholes. Working here sucks.

WHAT INSPIRED THIS STORY: *A slow night when I heard one of my tables talking about the sitcom* Three's Company.

An Open Letter to the Fork in the Trash Can

Dear Fork in the Trash Can,

I see you in there, peeking out from behind that piece of half-eaten fish and all those dirty bev naps. I'm sorry to see you in the trash can, but I think that is where you are going to stay. I'm not sure how you got there, but it must really suck to know that in a couple of hours, the trash bag will be tied up and dragged to the sidewalk, and there you will remain before you get

transported to a landfill, where everything around you decomposes. Sucks for you. You were probably on a plate as a server was scraping the remains of a grilled salmon into the garbage, and you slid right along for the ride. Did the server know it happened? Was that server me? The answer to both of those questions is yes.

I know that it's a bad thing to throw away silverware. This is why we constantly are running out of you. But why do you have to be so far down in the garbage? For me to save you, I'd have to reach deep into that nasty-ass garbage can and pull you out. If you were closer to the top I would consider it, but you are so far down there that if I were to retrieve you, my shirtsleeve might touch the inside of the trash bag, which is covered with ketchup, mashed potatoes, various sauces and gravies, some broccoli, a piece of fat trimmed from a New York shell steak, and some baby food that was left at Table 12. I can't take the chance that some of that disgustingness will get onto my impeccably clean uniform and require me to wash it sooner than I was planning to. Okay, let's be honest, fork: We both know that my uniform is nowhere close to being impeccably clean, but it's dirty enough already, so why should I take the chance of making it even more gross? I suppose I could roll my sleeve up and then reach in, but the thought of that restaurant slime getting onto my bare skin makes me want to hurl. Okay, let's be honest, fork: We both know that if I hurl, it's because I had five cocktails last night.

I'm sorry, fork. Just last week we had a shift meeting, and one of the things that came up was how we never have enough silverware. The manager told us that he thinks it's because we are being careless and tossing it out with the garbage. We servers told him that it's because customers are stealing it. Now that I see you in the trash can, I fear that the manager may have been right. What if he walks by and happens to look into the garbage and sees you there? He will gloat and then yell at us and call us lazy servers. We can't have that happen, and I know a way to make sure it won't. I will get a bunch of paper towels and toss them on top of you, so that no one will know you are there. I don't want you to be lonely, so I am going to give you a soup spoon and a knife for company. While I'm at it, I am also going to throw away three or four ketchup bottles that are getting close to being empty. Rather than refilling them, I'd rather just see them in the trash can next to you, fork. Once all that other crap is on top of you, you will be hidden from view forever.

Good-bye, fork, soup spoon, and knife. Ten minutes from now, when Table 16 gets his soup and I don't have a clean spoon to give him, I may regret this action. I might have to grab a dirty spoon and wash it by hand, but that's a chance I'm willing to take. If only you would have been closer to the top of the garbage, I could have saved you. But you aren't. You are all the way at the bottom, just barely visible. So near yet so very, very far away. So in the garbage you will stay. Thank you for your service, and I pray that you understand why I can't help you. My only hope is that you are one of *those forks that we use to shimmy open the paper towel dispenser and one of your tines is all bent up, in which case you deserve to be in the garbage. Farewell, fork. You served us well.*

Mustard and mayo,

The Bitchy Waiter

WHAT INSPIRED THIS STORY: *I really hate reaching into the trash can.*

I Served Olive Oyl

Have you ever wondered what Olive Oyl would look like in this day and age? Wonder no more, because she is sitting at Table 18 at the club. She has put on some weight, which is a good thing because I always thought Olive Oyl was a bit too thin. It was rumored that she had body dysmorphic disorder and may have had some type of eating disorder as well, which would explain why she always seemed to weigh about seventy pounds. Judging from her fickle nature, not being able to decide between Popeye and Bluto, it also appears that she probably has some issues with low self-esteem, but tonight she seems healthy and robust, as if she has finally gotten her life on track. Her hair is still jet black (obviously dyed), but she's in her early nineties, so more power to her. It also appears that she has gotten a boob job because she actually has breasts now. Popeye and Bluto probably chipped in after years of sharing pancake breakfasts. Her feet are still huge, but she is wearing snow boots, so maybe that is an illusion. Her sad black pencil skirt and red top have been jazzed up with a zebra-print jacket. Overall, she looks good for a ninety-year-old cartoon character.

"Hello, ma'am. May I get you something to drink?" I ask.

"Oh dear, I dunno. Oooh I dunno. Oooh . . . oooh."

"I can come back in a few minutes if you want to take a moment to decide."

"Nooo, I'm ready. Oooh, I would like a vodka on the rocks with olives. A *lot* of olives. I *love* olives."

"More than three?"

"Oooh, are they the big olives or the little olives? I love olives."

"They are the big olives," I say.

Olive Oyl smiles from ear to ear and says, "Oooh, I love the big olives. I'll take as many as you can give me."

I go back to the bar and cram five olives onto the tiny toothpick and carry it back to the table, along with her vodka. She eyes the glass and goes straight for the olives.

"Oooh dear, these *are* big olives. Thank you so much. I love olives," she says again as she swallows two of them at once.

"Yes, I heard that about you. Would you like to order any food, or will you be having olives for dinner tonight?" I follow the remark with a laugh, so she will think I am being funny and not bitchy, even though I am being bitchy and not funny.

"Oooh dear. Hmmm. Oooh my. Oh, I know! I would like an order of spinach artichoke dip."

If you say the word "extra," there will probably be an up charge.

Apparently, her years with Popeye have rubbed off on her, and she is a big fan of the spinach can. I am hesitant to ask her about Popeye—he was older than Olive Oyl, so he's probably dead now. I also want to ask her who the hell Swee'Pea was and if he was the bastard child of Popeye or Bluto. I almost share with her how, during the summer of '87, I played Olive Oyl at Elitch Gardens Theme Park in Denver. (If you were one of the hundreds of guys who gave Olive Oyl a hug that summer, it was me you were hugging and not a woman.)

The rest of the night with Olive Oyl is uneventful. She has her two-drink minimum and enjoys the show. She gives me a good tip and goes on her way. I am just happy to see that Olive Oyl is alive and well and living in New York City. Now if I could only find out whatever happened to Josie and the Pussycats . . .

> **WHAT INSPIRED THIS STORY:** *If a customer looks like a cartoon character, I am going to treat her like one.*

Jesus H. Christ on a Cracker

For God so loved the world, that he gave his only begotten Son, that whosoever believes in Him should not perish, but have everlasting life; and that Son shall also sit at Booth 16 and be served by the Bitchy Waiter.

—John 3:16½

I am about 99.9 percent sure that Jesus came into my restaurant. He certainly looked like Jesus. I have always heard that Jesus is everywhere, but I never expected him to show up in my station. I first see Him looking into the window of the restaurant. Initially, I think He is checking out the menu, but then I realize He must be seeing if there are any sinners inside who need saving. I suppose that's why He sat in my station. Jesus is fatter than I thought He would be, but He carries the weight well. I am a little

Do unto waitresses as you would have them do unto you.

nervous when I approach His table because I haven't been to church since 1988, when I woke up one Sunday morning in college feeling like going back to church after a three-year absence. I went to the nearest Baptist church, and the sermon that day happened to be about how being gay was a sin. "Oh, that's why I quit coming here," I thought, and headed right back out. But Jesus seems cool, and He doesn't even mention anything about how long it's been since He's heard from me.

He is with a lady friend. I assume it is Mary Magdalene, but she may have just been some casual encounter and I don't ask. I tell them the specials, and when He starts to talk I begin having my doubts that this guy is really Jesus because His voice is high-pitched and kind of un-Jesus-y. *"Maybe it's just some hipster dude who needs to shave and get a haircut,"* I think, but when he asks for a glass of red wine, I put that idea to rest. I consider bringing him a glass of water and letting him do his Jesus-magic, but then I figure it's His night out and maybe He doesn't feel like doing any tricks. Mary orders white zinfandel, which I think is a real slap in the face to Jesus. I serve the drinks, and they tell me they want a little time to decide before placing their order and then ask me for some bread.

"How many loaves would you like?" I ask Him.

"Ummm, just one," He says. "If we want more, we'll let you know."

"Just one? Not forty?" I wink at Him to let him know that I know if He wants more bread, He doesn't have to ask me for it. "Would you like any fishes with that?"

Jesus looks at me like he has heard this joke a hundred times, so I chill out and let Him have some space. I want to see if I can get Him to walk on water, so the next time I am near His table, I spill a glass of it on the floor next to Him. I pretend to clean it all up, but I leave some there just in case He gets up to go take a pee and floats over it. After what seems like forty days and forty nights, He finally calls me over to order. He asks for a shell steak, medium rare, and I am totally surprised. For some reason I just thought that Jesus would be a vegan, or a vegetarian, or at least a *pescatarian*. Mary orders the chicken breast, which doesn't surprise me at all because we all know how Mary Magdalene is, and, of course, she wants something with the word "breast" in it. Whore.

When their food is ready, I give Jesus extra ketchup for his fries because I want to see if he will pour it all over his plate and then part it like the Red Sea, but he doesn't even eat it at all. Way to disappoint, Jesus.

By this time, the restaurant is closed, and I am ready for the two of them to be on their way, but they keep on yapping about who knows what. When He finally does get up to go the bathroom, I'm not paying attention, so I don't know if He floats over the water or not. I place their check on the table, and when He hands me His credit card, His hand accidentally touches mine. I feel the warmth and power of His spirit flow into my body and right up my arm, through my chest, into my neck and directly to my face and lips, where it culminates in a tingly sensation. The two of them leave the restaurant and bless everyone as they walk through.

I go to clear their table and see what kind of tip Jesus and Mary left me. The tip is 15 percent, which is fine, but I expected a little more, considering how many dollars I had dropped into the church collection plate during the early to mid-1980s. I pick up the credit card slip to see what Jesus's autograph looks like, and then I notice the name on the card. The name is not Jesus. It is something like Robert or Michael. Hmmm,

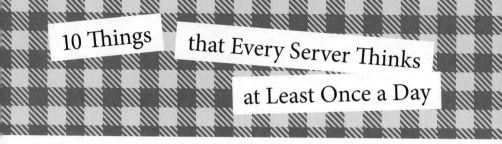

10 Things that Every Server Thinks at Least Once a Day

1. I wonder what grad school would be like.

2. If those parents don't care about their kid, then neither do I.

3. How much damage could I do with a butter knife?

4. Something stinks. Oh, wait—it's my uniform.

5. I need these old people to get out of my section.

6. Lemme just eat this real quick before my manager sees me.

7. Maybe I could just hide in the walk-in refrigerator for fifteen minutes.

8. I need a drink.

9. People suck.

10. I just want to get the fuck out of here.

could this guy have been a Jesus impersonator? Maybe he really was just some dude with long scraggly hair, a beard, and sandals. After all, I never saw this guy do any miracles. I put the credit card voucher into my apron and carry on with my closing sidework. When I get home, I look into the mirror and I notice something about my face. That morning, there was the very beginning of a cold sore making its debut on my lower lip, but now it is gone. Could it be that the touch from the Maybe-Jesus-Guy had cured my cold sore in much the same way he had cured those lepers? I think it's possible.

So, yes, I will stand behind my claim (99.9 percent) that Jesus sat in my station at Booth 16. The other .01 percent is reserved for the possibility that it was a guy from Williamsburg, Brooklyn named Robert or Michael who needed a shower and a damn haircut, and the cold sore was cured by the ointment in my pocket.

> **WHAT INSPIRED THIS STORY:** *Some greasy hipster sat in my station and ordered a glass of wine.*

Martha, the Patron Saint of Waiters

Hey, bitches. It's me, Martha. I'm the Patron Saint of Waiters and Waitresses. Most people call me St. Martha, but you can just call me Martha. I mean, I'm a saint and everything, but it's not as if I think I'm better than any of you. I'll bet a lot of you didn't even know you *had* a patron saint, did you? Well, you do, but I have a terrible publicist. It's really not that big a deal to be a saint. There's even a patron saint for finding a damn parking spot, for Christ's sake. You can read all about me on my Wikipedia page, but it's unauthorized, and I want to give you the real deal here.

So, yes, I served Jesus. He used to show up with his disciples, and I would serve him with my sister, Tabitha. He was pretty cool. They all used to come into the pub I worked in, but the owner eventually kicked them out because they would just order water, which Jesus would turn into wine. He would also ask for one basket of bread and then multiply it over and over again. They'd sit there for like four hours, talking. Judas would always grab the check and say, "Oh, I'll take care of it. I like to leave a 100 percent tip." Then he'd look at the bill and see that it was for nothing and say, "Hmmm, let's see . . . 100 percent of zero is . . . ZERO!" He thought he was so funny,

that Judas. He could be a real dick sometimes. The only time I got a decent tip was when Matthew, the tax collector, left me a coin of Tiberius. I took it home with me and we used it to buy a grain of rice that we ate for dinner.

So, anyway, after my boss told them they weren't allowed to take up any more tables unless they were going to start ordering things, I told them they could meet in my place. I don't know what I was thinking. I lived in a tiny mud hut that I shared with my sister, my parents, five brothers, two goats, and a donkey, but they took me up on the offer. I think I mostly did it because one of Jesus's disciples was really cute. His name was Thomas, but he barely even noticed that I was there. They would meet once a week and talk about the future and the glory of God and blah, blah, blah. I tried to pay attention but I was always busy filling their water goblets so Jesus could make them some more wine. Once they got started, they could really guzzle it down.

One time, I sat down at the table because I was interested in a story that Jesus was telling, but Peter told me that women weren't allowed to sit with the disciples. Then he told me to get him some more water. I told him that his teeth were stained red and I didn't think he needed any more "water," but he denied me a third time and shooed me away from the table. What an SOB.

I was with them all at their Last Supper. You can't see me in the famous painting because, of course, I was busy working. That Last Supper was held at a banquet hall they rented. I volunteered to work it because I knew that something big was about to go down, and I wanted to see Jesus one more time. And Thomas, too. They were all sad that day. I'll never forget what Jesus told me that last time I saw him. He leaned over to me and said, "Martha, I will pray for you that you might serve better. I will help you to overcome your distractions and worries and be present to become a better waitress." I thanked him but didn't have the heart to say that waiting tables was just my side job until I got my big break as an actress. That was the last time I ever saw Jesus.

I never did get my big break, but I continued serving. Before long, I became the best waitress the land of Galilee ever did see. I eventually opened my own wine bar, known as Martha's Vineyard, which was very successful. After I died, a local bishop suggested that I be canonized, and the next thing I knew, I was Martha, the patron saint of servants, including waiters and waitresses. I was very surprised and honored. Would I like to be the patron saint of actresses, like that tramp St. Pelagia? Sure I would, but at least I'm not the patron saint of mad cow disease or something.

The next time you are at work and begin to feel stressed out, just take a second to think of me, Martha. I am your patron saint, and I am here to help you feel better. I will not, however, help you bus your tables. I'm done with that shit.

WHAT INSPIRED THIS STORY: *My friend Marlene, a good Catholic girl, told me about this very important saint.*

The Real Story of the First Thanksgiving

Thursday, November 25, 1621. My name is Squantette and I'm exhausted. I'm working a catering gig all day today. My uncle owns a catering company called Squanto's Special Events, and he is short-staffed today so he begged me to help out. I didn't want to do it, but after he offered me some beads, a hatchet, and two potatoes, here I am.

It is down at Plymouth Plantation, and all these Pilgrims are celebrating some harvest or something. They think because they learned how to grow freakin' corn that all their troubles are over. Please, the only reason they even *know* how to grow corn is because Uncle Squanto taught them. He taught them how to catch eel, too, but these sorry-ass Pilgrims don't cook it right. Eel is best when it's cooked on a spit over the open flame, but they boil it and then chop it up and mix it with some kind of cream or milk. They call it a "dip." It looks nasty.

I had to get here really early and help Mrs. Winslow get everything set up. First off, she's made me put a bunch of tables together and then cover

THAT'S NOT MY SIDEWORK.

them with blankets. It looks stupid to me, but hey—I'm getting beads, a hatchet, and two potatoes. Whatever you want, lady. Then she has me washing potatoes and carrots, which makes no sense to me at all. They were just pulled from the ground, which is the cleanest thing I know, but she's making me carry them all the way to the river and rinse them off. As I dip them into the water, I watch a cow take a piss in the river right upstream from me and then I see one of their stupid little dogs playing in the water. But sure, no problem: I'll wash the potatoes and carrots.

When I get back, she wants help making something called a pumpkin pie. Now I love me some pumpkin, but once she starts mixing it with sugar and milk, I lose my appetite. So, yeah, basically, I just help her all morning by taking perfectly good food and watching her fuck it up.

By about Shadow Hitting Big Rock time, people all start to gather around the tables that are covered in blankets. They all sit down and start bossing me around, like they've totally forgotten that I have lived here since I was born, and their asses have only been here for like 13 Moons or something. Uncle Squanto shows up at this time to make sure everything is under control. When he gets there, I notice a few Pilgrims treating him like he isn't the one who helped their bony asses make it through last winter. Most of these Pilgrims are nice, but some of them just seem a little "dodgy" to me. Turns out Uncle Squanto and some of his friends get a place at one of the tables. I do notice that it isn't the *main* table, but a smaller one over to the side where all the kids are sitting. Typical. They want us to be one of them but not *too much* one of them.

Mrs. Winslow and I are running around trying to get all the food finished, and by this point I am beginning to wonder if Uncle Squanto is paying me enough. This is hard work. They have squash, turnips, onions, fowl, venison, "eel dip," clams, smoked fish, and about a million desserts. When we finally get everything onto the table, Mr. Crackstone (I can't even with that name . . .) stands up to make a speech. I paraphrase:

We come together on this day with our families and our friends, both new and old, for we are here to give thanks for all we have been given. We owe this debt to God but also to Squanto, who has been our teacher and our adviser since we have come to this new land. We have endured much hardship and we know there is more ahead of us, but for today, let us be thankful for what we have. We share this bounty with our neighbors, the Indians, and we hope that we can continue to learn from them and that we can give them something in return. We break this bread with gratitude and thanks.

So yeah, it is a pretty nice speech, except that he calls us "Indians," and I guess he forgot that they have already given us plenty. Thanks for the smallpox, Pilgrims. It's really great.

About halfway through the meal, Mrs. Winslow makes me a plate of food and tells me to sit down and take a break. I taste the eel dip, and, I have to say, it is pretty good. When everyone is finished, we all clean up together and then sit around and watch the kids play games. There's talk about doing this every year, and I would love to have the day off to enjoy it with *my* family. That is, unless Uncle Squanto is willing to give me more beads, *two* hatchets, and *three* potatoes next year. Actually, this so-called Thanksgiving might be a good day to make some quick bank.

WHAT INSPIRED THIS STORY: *Having to cater waiter on Thanksgiving for five straight years.*

A Sweaty Wonderland

It is July and New York City is in the midst of its first heat wave of the season, our third day of 97-degree temperatures. For those of you living in Texas and Arizona, I realize that 97 degrees is what you look forward to after a 115-degree scorcher, but here in New York City, that is freakin' hot. And at two of my three jobs, the air-conditioning is having challenges. (In corporate speak, "challenges" means "big fucking problems.")

On one of these hot days, I am at the restaurant where the A/C is weak even on days when the sun isn't reaching through the ozone layer and molesting me. When I get to work, I know that I had better set up the patio because, despite the heat, some masochistic asshole will think it's a nice idea to sit out there. Three hours into the shift, it seems as if I have wasted my time because nobody is interested in sitting in a sauna while eating a hamburger. And then it happens: A woman comes in, eyeballing the patio.

"Is the backyard open?" she asks.

"Yes, it is. Would you like to sit outside?"

"Is it hot out there?"

Now, this lady just stepped in from the blazing heat and wants to know if it is hot outside. My nerves are already short because of the lack of A/C, and my brain is a bit frozen from spending every spare moment with my head in the walk-in cooler.

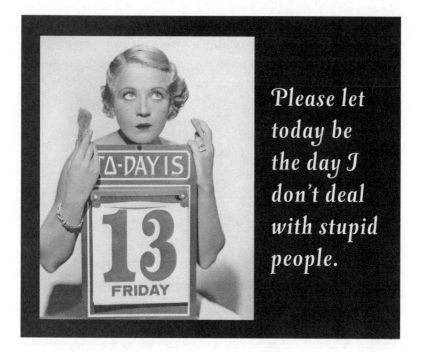

TŌ-DAY IS

13

FRIDAY

Please let today be the day I don't deal with stupid people.

"It's the same heat back there that you just came in from." I smile at her in an effort to hide that I think she is an idiot.

"Well, can we go back and see if it feels any different?"

"Yes, ma'am. Sure we can." I grab a menu and lead her to the depths of hell we call a patio.

I open the French doors and step outside. I am surprised at how different it feels from when I had last been out there three hours before. The air is crisp, almost chilly. I look around and notice a thin layer of frost on the metallic tabletops. As I stand there, I feel the temperature dip twenty degrees, and then another ten. In the back corner of the patio, the evergreen tree is decorated for Christmas, and two partridges are making a nest in it. Sitting at one of the tables is Santa Claus and Jack Frost, each with a steaming cup of hot chocolate.

"You're not allowed to bring outside food and beverages here, sir," I say to Santa.

"Ho, ho, ho," he laughs. "We didn't see a server so we brought our own. I do apologize."

He touches the side of his nose with his stubby mitten-covered thumb, and the two paper cups disappear. "We are waiting for two more friends. Could we get menus, young man?"

"I'm just drinking," says Jack Frost. "Bring me a hot toddy."

"Can you say 'please'?" says Santa.

Jack Frost rolls his eyes. "Please."

Two figures brush past us, and I recognize Frosty the Snowman and Mrs. Claus. They pull up two chairs and join the table. Frosty has an icicle hanging off his ass, and Mrs. Claus is wrapped up in a scarf that has images of children sledding down a hill.

"Dear," she says to her husband. "Frosty is warm. Can't you do something about this heat? It must be forty degrees out here. Look at him; poor thing's starting to melt. That icicle wasn't there ten minutes ago."

Santa again touches his nose with his thumb, and immediately the wind blows in from the north, bringing with it snowflakes.

"Where's my fucking hot toddy?" yells Jack Frost.

I am so mesmerized by what is happening on the patio that I have forgotten I am at work. I look at the woman who had wanted to sit outside. Her cheeks are red with the cold air and a tiny bit of mucus is slipping out of her nose. I hand her a tissue, and she shivers as she wipes the snot away. I hear jingle bells overhead and look up to see Rudolph along with eight pigs flying above us and pulling a sleigh.

"Oh, God, it's hot out here too," says the lady. "I'll just sit inside, I guess."

"Good idea," I reply.

WHAT INSPIRED THIS STORY: *A woman who doesn't understand how weather works.*

The Softer Side of Bitch

THERE'S A NEW GIRL IN TOWN

I am at my place of employment—a music venue where I serve drinks while singers perform—but this time I'm a patron, not an employee. Sometimes the show is good, sometimes the show is bad, and sometimes the show reaches deep into my soul, finds my tiny hardened heart, and makes it break a little.

Tonight I am watching Linda Lavin, best known for her iconic role as Alice Hyatt on CBS's *Alice*, which ran from 1976 to 1985. Of course, I loved the show. Too many people don't know that Linda Lavin is also an accomplished singer and Broadway actress with a Tony Award and many nominations. Ms. Lavin had done a show at my club years before I worked there, and every time I saw the poster of it that still hangs in the lobby, I felt a pang of longing. When I learned that she was doing another show, I almost peed myself. Could it be that I was going to get to see this woman in person? The same woman whose sitcom I watched on TV every week through junior high and high school?

When I get to the club, I am surrounded by famous people who have come to see Ms. Lavin work her magic. The lights dim and a voice comes over the speaker. "Ladies and gentleman . . . Linda Lavin!"

There she is—not five feet from me—smiling, tossing her hair, and scanning the crowd for her friends. *"Oh, look at me!"* I think. *"I'm right here. Make eye contact with me. Please, no one wants to be here more than I do!"* She starts to sing her first song, and the night begins to melt away into a fog of sense memory. Her mannerisms are the same as they were when she made a smart remark to Mel, the owner of the diner her character worked in. But this isn't Alice Hyatt; this is Linda Lavin. And then she sings the theme song to *Alice*. I know it's silly, but I start to cry. All of a sudden I am twelve years old again, laughing at Vera with an exploding box of straws and thinking that Alice is such a cool mom and that Flo is so funny. The next song she sings is called "The Song Remembers When."

Music has the power to transport you to another time. To this day, whenever I hear the song "I Melt with You," I float back to 1986, to Judith's living room, where we are watching a slide show that my best friends in college put together. I can't hear that song without feeling nostalgic, happy, and incredibly sad all at the same time.

She has a lot of wonderful things to tell her audience. "Fear is your friend," she says when talking about the nervousness that we all experience on occasion and must use to our advantage. "I love my life," she exclaims. "My life is a big surprise to me." She is so grateful to still be working, and she wants to remind us all to be thankful for the moments that we receive on a daily basis. I know she only played a waitress on television, but it feels like we are wearing the same apron.

After the show is over, my cheeks hurt from smiling. I rub the tears out of my eyes and go to the lobby to see her greeting guests under the poster of her show from three years before—the same poster that has taunted me since I began working here. I have already forgotten her advice about fear and walk past her, too afraid to shake her hand and thank her for the evening—and so much more. Why didn't I? I wish I would have told her this: *Ms. Lavin, I know you hear this all the time, but I loved Alice. I'm a waiter and you gave the character of Alice such realness. She was never ashamed of her job because she knew that waiting tables wasn't her life. Alice was a singer who waited tables. I am a writer who waits tables. Thank you. Your show tonight moved me more than you could ever know.*

Many months pass, and I am working a show for a very established singer who has been in the business for a million years. Her shows always bring out celebrities, and tonight is no exception. On the far side of the room is Linda Lavin. Technically, she isn't in my station, but I walk past her once, and she asks me for a cup of black coffee and some water. Of course, I am more than eager to get it for her, and I decide at that moment that I am going to let fear be my friend and talk to her before the evening is finished.

After the show is over, I keep my eye on Ms. Lavin, waiting for just the right moment to approach her. I hate being that needy fan, but I don't want to regret not telling her how much her performance had inspired me. As she slowly inches toward the exit, I see her constantly being stopped by other people. I don't want to join that queue, but I have to. As her hand is on the door to leave, I seize my chance.

"Excuse me, Ms. Lavin? I hate to bother you but I must tell you that I saw your cabaret a few months ago and I truly loved it. I just wanted you to know that."

I think my voice is an octave higher than normal, which is *really high* because whenever I am on the phone with a stranger, they always call me "ma'am."

"Oh, thank you, that's very nice," she says.

Oh my God, Linda Lavin is talking to me. Linda Lavin is talking to me. This is it. I have peaked.

"I wrote a story about it and posted it on my blog, 'The Bitchy Waiter.'"

Oh my God, am I really pimping out my blog to Linda Lavin? Yes. Yes, I am.

At this point, it gets a little fuzzy. Ms. Lavin's eyes light up with recognition.

"Was that you?" she asks as she grabs my hand.

Oh my God, Linda Lavin is holding my hand. Linda freakin' Lavin is holding my hand that I should have washed before I came to talk to her because I think it might be sticky. I am about to pass out right here with a stack of check presenters in my arms, and credit cards are going to go all over the place, but I don't care because Linda Lavin is holding my freaking hand!

"I read that story!" she continues. "I loved it. You're a very good writer. Thank you."

Oh my God, that's it. I'm done. Linda Lavin didn't just call me a writer; she called me a "good writer." Someone hold me, because I am about to fall over and head right up to Jesus. Jesus, look at the menu because I am on my way to take your order and get you a basket of bread!

I make a conscious decision to let go of her hand, so I don't "accidentally" break her fingers off and stuff them into my apron as mementos.

"Thank you very much. You just made my night. It's nice to meet you," I tell her.

"It's nice to meet you, too," she says.

And with that, she drifts out of my life.

It was a good night to be a waiter. A good night, indeed. Sometimes the apron I wear allows me moments like this one. Thank you, apron. And thank you, Linda Lavin.

The only thing sweeter than dessert is punching out with a shift drink in a paper cup and a pocket full of cash.

dessert

noun. • The sweet course eaten at the end of the meal. The ending.

WORKING IN RESTAURANTS FOR THE BETTER part of two decades has done a lot for me. True, it has given me a lifelong disdain of lemons in water, but there are many positive aspects that have come out of slinging hash for this many years. As I get older, I realize that many of the things I have learned in restaurants have carried over to my regular life and made me a better person.

Have you ever had to wait on someone you really didn't want to? No, I don't mean that lady with the cold sores all over her mouth or that gaggle of stroller moms. I'm talking about someone you knew, someone you wanted to impress. It can be awkward when people from another part of your life turn up in your station, and suddenly you are their lackey.

Many years ago when I worked in Houston on Highway 290, someone came into my station whom I recognized from high school. Let's call him Guy. Guy was Mr. High School. He was a smart, popular, handsome cheerleader, and he dated the girl that I thought I was in love with. He was everything I wanted to be, and he made me sick in that jealous, I-want-your-life kinda way. And suddenly he is sitting in my section and I have to go ask him if wants rolls or cornbread.

I look down at my uniform and notice the gravy and butter stains on it, and then I look at Guy, who is wearing a suit and tie and sitting with three other men in business attire. My mind travels back to the day when we are having our school photos taken. Guy is wearing this really cool purple sweater that I covet, and I am wearing a stupid-ass T-shirt because I had forgotten about the school photos.

"Can someone please take Table 23 for me? I can't do it."

"Why? You're not even busy. It's four men in suits. You don't want it?"

I just can't do it. I am embarrassed. After high school, I went to college in another state to study theater and make it as an actor. Years passed, and I am back in Texas, waiting tables. And here is Guy, in a suit, during the lunch rush. In my mind, wearing a suit and going to lunch at noon meant success. He certainly isn't a waiter. When he leaves, I watch him drive away in his fancy Chrysler LeBaron, which he had parked right next to my old Honda Civic. I go into the bathroom to splash some reality on my face and move on with my day. I feel like a loser. A gravy-stained, chicken fried steak–smelling loser.

That was years ago. I have changed. Yes, I still wait tables, and as much as I bitch about it, I know the reason I do it. I do it because I still remember what I wanted to be when I grew up: an actor or a writer. If Guy came into my station now, I would be proud to wait on him because I would be able to say that I am still pursuing my dream. It may not look like I have that much success to someone who is ordering a cocktail from me, but I know that the level of success I have surpasses many others in this world. Just the fact that I still dream and hope says a lot about me. Guy might be a lawyer or a banker or some other bullshit boring-ass profession like that, but I am what I always wanted to be: an actor and a writer—one who supplements his income by waiting tables, but an actor and a writer nonetheless. So today, let all of us servers be proud of ourselves for doing what we do. We have this job that allows us to make a decent living and it also gives us the opportunity to do other things. We can continue our educations, we can take extra days off, we can pick up shifts if we want to make extra money, we don't have to think about our jobs once we punch out, and we can carry a tray like nobody's fucking business. On top of all that, being a server has taught me several lessons that I make use of when I am not wearing an apron:

- **SAVE FOR A RAINY DAY.** When most of your income depends on fluctuating tips, you get pretty good at holding onto money once you have it. A really great Friday night shift, where you walk home with $250, can be followed by a Saturday morning shift during a blizzard where no one comes in and you only make twenty bucks. Waiting tables has taught me how to count my pennies and save what I make, because you never know when the financial rug will be pulled out from under you. (Unless you are wearing your slip-resistant shoes when that happens, it's easy to fall down.)

- **MAKE SMALL TALK.** Going into any situation where you are surrounded by strangers can be difficult. Whether it's a party, a new job, or a meeting, the first impression you make is a lasting one. Being a waiter has given me the skills to make conversation with all sorts of people and make a great first impression. It's as easy as asking them how they would like their burger cooked. When all else fails, compliment their outfits.

- **DON'T SWEAT THE SMALL STUFF.** There was a time when I was a newbie, and I would run into the kitchen to hide until the burger for Table 12 was ready. One day, an older server told me something I will never forget: "It's just lunch. There will be another one tomorrow, and there is no such thing as a lunch emergency." I have carried that calming thought outside the restaurant. When I am stuck on the train or in traffic or in a long line at the store, all I have to remember is that this is probably not a very big deal in the grand scheme of things.

- **BE A TEAM PLAYER.** A restaurant staff is ever-changing. People come and go, and you never know whom you will be working with during any given shift. Because of that, some days you work with people you like, and some days you work with people you don't. But working in a restaurant requires teamwork—especially when it's slammed with a church group who all showed up on the same bus at the same time, and they want thirty-seven separate checks, even though everyone ordered the exact same thing. Whether you like everyone or not, you still may need to ask other servers to water your table, and they might ask you to take some bread somewhere. You quickly figure out that it's much easier to just get along than it is to bitch at each other. Suck it up: You're a member of the team.

- **PRIORITIZE.** Having a station full of people all needing things at the same time is a real lesson in making the best use of your time. If Table 1 needs to have their cocktails rung in, and Table 2 needs more water, and Table 3 needs spoons for their dessert that will be up any minute, you get real good at figuring out which one is the most important. (The spoons. Duh. Unless, of course, the cocktails are ready and the bartender wants you to taste-test them for quality control. In that case, cocktails take immediate precedence.)

- **MULTITASK.** This goes right along with prioritizing. If you ring in the drinks and then grab the water pitcher on your way to the sidestand to get spoons, you can then drop the spoons at Table 3, fill the waters at Table 2, and then breeze by Table 1 to tell them their drinks are on the way. This is handy in the real world, like when you are at the liquor store to pick up supplies for margaritas. If you walk down the aisle and see the rum, you may as well buy it then, because you might want daiquiris tomorrow.

- **A SMILE WILL GET YOU FAR IN LIFE.** When someone sits in my station with a sourpuss look and then tells me he wants the happy-hour price for his beer, even though happy hour ended five minutes ago, I am not going to do it. By contrast, if someone smiles and asks nicely, it is very possible that I will hit the happy-hour beer price. A smile makes a huge difference, even if it's fake one, like mine.

- **BE HUMBLE.** Being in a position of subservience really teaches you how to treat others. When I am treated poorly, it's very obvious that this person is used to having people to push around. I know what it's like to be told what to do without a "please" or a "thank you." When I am out in the real world, I make certain that I always make eye contact with anyone who is doing something for me, and I make frequent use of "please" and "thank you."

- **BE PATIENT.** It's not easy to have patience when a three-year-old at your table wants to order for herself. The mom is saying, "You can do it, honey. Tell the man what you want," but I can feel the stares of the four other tables that need my attention as well. When your income depends on how patient and attentive you are, you learn patience quickly. That's why when I am at the grocery store, in the 10 ITEMS OR LESS checkout line, stuck behind a senior citizen who has fifteen items, I know to breathe deeply and let it go.

- **WEAR GOOD SHOES.** I am on my feet all day, so the shoes I wear are very important to my health and well-being. Cheap shoes don't support your soles, and they fall apart too soon. Waiting tables has taught me to spend the extra twenty-five bucks for the better shoes. They last longer, they look better, and they will save you a lot of backaches and ankle blisters. But they will always look like restaurant shoes.

I look back at how long I have been in the food and beverage industry and realize it has been more than half my life. From my first job as a dishwasher in 1984, to my years as a busboy in college, to my first serving job in 1990, to last Thursday when I worked at the restaurant three blocks from my apartment, I have devoted my life to food service. How could I have known that so many years after my grandma Lillian helped me memorize the menu for my first job waiting tables I would still be making a living as a server? I am a bitchy waiter, but also a proud one. And all those Guys out

THE WORLD WOULD BE
A BETTER PLACE IF
EVERYONE WAITED TABLES
FOR ONE MONTH.

there? They can keep their Chrysler LeBarons. I have my dreams. Even if I never get that Tony Award I had planned on winning by the year 2000, or this book doesn't catapult me to the literary stratosphere, I have a lot of awesome memories from my life behind the menu. And maybe someday I will also develop a patented way of getting these damn ranch dressing stains out of my 100 percent polyester black fucking shirt that my employers made me pay for, even though they require me to wear it.

Image Credits

Alamy
© ClassicStock: 9, 220

© Darron Cardosa
50, 86, 113, 141, 191, 219

Depositphotos
© drakonova: 204; © everett225: 24, 41, 46, 100, 122, 124, 144, 211

Getty Images
© Mac Gramlich/Archive Photos: 179; © Bert Hardy Advertising Archive: 34; © Thurston Hopkins: 59; © Lambert: 97; © H. Armstrong Roberts/ClassicStock: 184; © Sickles Photo Reporting: 156; © SuperStock: 173, 208

iStockphoto
© HultonArchive: 44, 80, 83, 89, 92, 104, 130, 199

© Mark Alan Jones
231

Shutterstock
© Everett Collection: 1, 6, 12, 19, 21, 27, 32, 37, 65, 74, 102, 107, 120, 127, 132, 135, 137, 149, 153, 158, 161, 169, 182, 194, 197, 214, 227; © Retro-ClipArt: 16, 52, 55, 61, 70, 77, 110, 115, 147, 151, 175, 202

Acknowledgments

MY HUSBAND, MARK ALAN JONES: for loving me and for listening to the "Bitchy Waiter" since 2008.

MY PARENTS, LIONEL AND NELLIE CARDOSA: for always believing I could do anything.

RON SPENCE: for being my right-hand Bitchy Waiter.

MICHAEL FAZIO: for all the encouragement.

MARK WOLFE-WARNAKE: for finding and fixing so many of my grammar issues.

SCOTT KATZMAN: for letting me steal his phrase "dumb as a bag of hair."

JUDYTHE COHEN: for first convincing me that I could write a book.

MOLLY ROGERS AND MELISSA WILEY: for all the author advice.

KAT KINSMAN: for introducing me to my agent.

SCOTT MENDEL: for being my agent and making this happen.

MELANIE MADDEN: for making this book so much better than I ever could have done by myself.

LINDA LAVIN: for letting me write about her.

BILLY STRITCH: for connecting me with Linda Lavin.

LUCILLE ARAJ: for igniting the first flame of creativity when she put me in choir in the second grade.

About the Author

DARRON CARDOSA proudly refers to himself as a media whore, and has been known to spend hours at a time linking his blog to every conceivable website that may get him more traffic. *The Bitchy Waiter* blog now boasts over 10,000 followers on Twitter and over 250,000 fans on Facebook. In 2011 he was featured in a *New York Post* article entitled "Should You Trust Your Server?" He has been a guest on WOR talk radio and also on WNYC public radio. In August 2011 he appeared as a guest on *Dr. Phil* to discuss children's behavior in restaurants, and in November 2011 he was a contributing commentator for *CBS Sunday Morning*, which reached more than five million viewers. In August 2012 his blog was referenced in an article on CNN's website Eatocracy.com, and in August 2013 he did a segment called "Ask the Expert" for NBC's *Today Show*. Darron lives in New York, NY.